SHAKESPEARE'S
ADVICE TO
THE PLAYERS

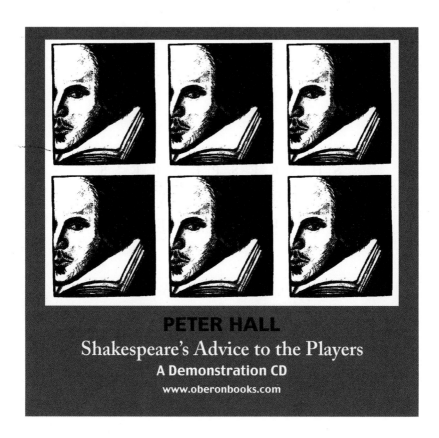

PETER HALL
Shakespeare's Advice to the Players
A Demonstration CD
www.oberonbooks.com

PETER HALL

SHAKESPEARE'S
ADVICE TO
THE PLAYERS

OBERON BOOKS
LONDON

First published in 2003 by Oberon Books Ltd
(incorporating Absolute Classics)
521 Caledonian Road, London N7 9RH
Tel: 020 7607 3637 / Fax: 020 7607 3629
e-mail: oberon.books@btinternet.com
website: www.oberonbooks.com

Paperback edition first published 2004

A catalogue record for this book is available from the British Library.

ISBN 1 84002 411 9

Cover design: Andrzej Klimowski and Jeff Willis

Proofread by Prufrock – www.prufrock.co.uk

Printed in Great Britain by Antony Rowe, Chippenham.

This book is dedicated to the memory of George Rylands and of F R Leavis;

also to John Barton, for fifty years my friend and colleague

THE MERCHANT OF VENICE, Peter Hall Company at the Phoenix Theatre 1989.
Dustin Hoffman as Shylock.

CONTENTS

ROMEO AND JULIET, Royal Shakespeare Company 1961.
Edith Evans as the Nurse.

ACKNOWLEDGEMENTS

In my fifty years as a director, I have worked on Shakespeare's text with hundreds of actors, from the greats – Ashcroft, Dench, Evans, Gielgud, Olivier, Scofield – to the beginners who were learning about verse and prose as they rehearsed the plays. I learned from them all, and I thank them all.

Many books have helped me, in particular *The Oxford Shakespeare* edited by Stanley Wells and Gary Taylor; David and Ben Crystal's book *Shakespeare's Words*; and *Shakespeare's Lives* by S Schoenbaum.

I am grateful for the support of James Hogan and his colleagues at Oberon Books – particularly to the graphic designers Andrzej Klimowski and Jeff Willis who have made considerable creative contributions to this book. Thanks are due also to Paul Groothuis for his help in the production of the CD and to Rebecca Hall and Daniel Stevens who participate in it.

I must particularly thank Roger Warren who cast an enthusiastic eye over the manuscript. More importantly, he prepared the Shakespeare extracts with minimum punctuation, a task he has performed for me on many stage productions.

I am grateful too to the archivists at the Royal Shakespeare Company, the Shakespeare Centre in Stratford-upon-Avon, and the Royal National Theatre; to all the photographers whose pictures are included in this book; and to Richard Pearson for the generous loan of photographs from his collection.

Finally without the assistance of Maggie Sedwards, this book would not exist; her help has been extraordinary.

PROLOGUE

Can we mount an authentic performance as Shakespeare would have seen it? No. Authenticity in the performing arts is ultimately impossible. We cannot perform anything, be it dance, music or drama, with any certainty either that we are performing in the right style (we are different people, with different attitudes and different sensibilities) or that we will understand even in approximately the same way as the original spectators.

The Shakespeare problem is particularly sensitive. Our language has changed, our accents have altered and our religious, political and social preoccupations have been transformed in the last 400 years. We are literally different people, in scale, appetite and morality.

In another 200 or so years, Shakespeare will only be faintly visible – rather as Chaucer is to us. Language must change or die. And Shakespeare's language will not always be readily comprehensible; he will soon need translating. A book like this will then be useless, because with the disappearance of the original words goes the disappearance of the form. It is also why translated Shakespeare is so much modified, if not simplified.

But for the moment we can pursue in Shakespeare (as we can in performing Baroque music) a creative compromise. If we understand the author's formal demands, we have some chance of representing them in modern terms. Of course performance fashions change; they must, in order to keep up with the subtle alterations in the audience's sensibilities. But an iambic beat is still an iambic beat; a legato phrase in Mozart is still a legato phrase. The speech doesn't need sentimental Victorian booming, or the music string-playing with a 19th century vibrato. The modern equivalent can be found providing we honour every part of the original that still speaks to us. What 2003 means by 'trippingly on the tongue' (which is to Hamlet's taste in his advice to the players) will become something very different by 2053. But it should still trip.

Nonetheless, there are major difficulties. I have done many productions of Shakespeare where the verse speaking has been highly praised by some critics and roundly condemned by others. Someone must have been wrong. The reason for these contradictions is that there are no accepted standards of verse speaking and not much agreement on the old rhetorical forms. Some people like emotional Shakespeare which is almost sung; some don't. Those who like the singing often think it is poetic. I like wit and restraint, and I believe Shakespeare liked them too. Hamlet again:

> **Speak the speech I pray you as I pronounced it**
> **to you, trippingly on the tongue; but if you**

**mouth it as many of your players do, I had as
lief the town crier had spoke my lines.**

Today, rhetoric is not trusted. It is no longer taught in schools, nor do most of us listen to its rhythms in a Sunday morning sermon. This is partly why there are no longer any accepted standards for verse speaking. Well-spoken productions don't usually get commented on: they are just thought of as good. It is the productions which don't communicate whose verse gets every kind of comment from the tolerant to the critical. I once read a critic who condemned an actor for his appalling verse speaking as Shylock in the Tubal scene. Clearly nobody had pointed out to him that in this scene Shylock and Tubal speak entirely in prose. The rhythm should be different.

In our society, to be rhetorical is a term of abuse. A hundred years ago a politician would depend on rhetoric in his public speeches in order to stress his points. He would use repetitions, balanced answering phrases and antitheses. It was his way of defining a clear and formal argument. Today politicians want to be seen on television, chatting away like any other man in the street, with as many 'you knows' and 'reallys' as they can muster. Informality is thought to be honest; formality is considered artificial and untrustworthy.

But if Shakespeare's form is observed, an audience is still held; if it is not observed, the audience's attention strays and strays very quickly. So Shakespeare lives. And if an actor *understands* a speech and expresses its meaning through the form, the audience will understand also, even if they might not understand if they read the speech through once to themselves.

These are difficult times for the classical actor because there is little technical consistency. I have worked in a theatre where the director before me urged the actors to run on from one line to the next, speak the text like prose, and to take breaths whenever they felt like it. He wanted them, he said, to be 'real'. They were; but they weren't comprehensible. I then arrived and said just the opposite – that the line structure was the main instrument of communication. Its five beats made up a phrase which was by and large as much as an audience could take in without a sense break.

In the past it was hardly necessary to train actors to speak verse. They had – all of them – been marinated in so much Shakespeare during their early years in regional theatres or on classical tours that the rhythm came naturally to them. It played in their heads all the time – like an insistent backing group. Young actors are now exposed to little

Shakespeare because most regional theatres cannot afford to do plays that require more than a dozen actors. And drama schools spend little time training young actors in Shakespeare because they know it is unlikely to be used in the professional theatre. Only a small percentage of actors will ever actually *do* Shakespeare and that will be because they have joined the Royal Shakespeare Company or the National Theatre. Shakespeare, it is thought, is of little use for the behavioural understatement of television acting. The fact that it is still the best training for any actor or any style is overlooked. There is no better way for an actor to train his intellect, his body, his breathing, his voice, and his skills in communicating with an audience than by playing Shakespeare. It is an Olympic course in acting. If the resulting performer is a rough and crude actor who is full of overstatement, then he is no true Shakespearean and he has not been well taught. He is distorting the form by overstating it. Shakespeare demands that we delicately fulfil it.

Some actors confuse verse with 'poetry' – which they take to be the indulgent and often sentimental use of high emotion to support lyrical lines. 'Purple passages' they may with justice call them. But verse is not necessarily 'poetical' or even 'purple'. And it certainly isn't in Shakespeare. The main purpose of his verse is to represent ordinary speech and tell a story lucidly. At its best, it is quick and clear. And if it is delivered with five accents as written, and with a tiny sense break (*not* a stop) at the end of each line, communication with an audience is immediate. That is why Shakespeare wrote in iambic pentameters; he didn't want to be 'poetic', he wanted to be understood. He earns his poetry and his metaphors when the emotions become intense. He can then move from plain speech to intricate images with ease. And he is able to use the most banal things – Lear's button, or Cleopatra's corset – to break our hearts. Most of his great moment are based on the mundane and the concrete, rather than the hyperbolical.

SHAKESPEARE'S ADVICE TO THE PLAYERS

Speaking Shakespeare's verse and prose is an easily learned technique. It takes about three days for an actor to familiarise himself with what he has to look for; and it takes a few weeks more for him to become comfortable in the techniques.

Shakespeare tells the actor when to go fast and when to go slow; when to come in on cue, and when to accent a particular word or series of words. He tells the actor much else; and he always tells him *when* to do it (provided the actor knows where to look). But he never tells him *why*. The motive, the *why*, remains the creative task of the actor. He has to endorse feelings in himself which support the form that Shakespeare's text has given him. For instance, the words may tell the actor to speak slowly because they are monosyllabic; but they will not tell him *why*. The actor's emotions must do that. A measured speech must be credible because it is supported by the appropriate emotion; otherwise it will seem imposed and unreal. But this gives the actor an almost infinite number of choices. And, once achieved, form and feeling interreact on each other and become one. So form comes first and, if it is observed, it helps provoke the feeling.

There are some fifty actors who practise this technique in Britain and there are a handful of directors. Many of this select band are of the older generation and know how to do it simply because they performed so much Shakespeare in their youth. Some might be hard put to tell you the techniques. They shape the structure of the lines and the rhythms naturally, almost without thinking. Many of the younger actors are eager to learn, but they can easily be put off by the sound of the technical terms or the indifference of directors. Demystification and practice are, as usual, the main needs. When all the analysis has been done, speaking Shakespeare is like riding a bicycle or skating at the local ice rink – it suddenly happens.

Actors quickly understand that, if they know the technique, they have a better chance to make the text work. They are empowered then to make the audience listen and understand. This desire to achieve the form is weaker in directors, perhaps because they sometimes feel (wrongly in my opinion) that they are being forced into old patterns rather than allowed to pursue the new. Yet they need to understand that even though a musical phrase has a number of defined and unalterable notes, it is capable of infinite variety; it can express anything. The same is true of a line of Shakespeare's. But neither those who put on the plays nor those who study the plays have recognised how much Shakespeare tells us about his form, and therefore *how* he should be performed. Scholarship over the centuries has paid little attention to Shakespeare's verse structure or to the balance of his prose. But then scholarship, I suppose, has usually been dealing with the written rather than the spoken word. With few exceptions, scholarship *reads* the text, it does not *hear* it.

I have been trying to direct Shakespeare for over fifty years. What I have recorded in this book are not techniques that I have invented; I have been taught them by others as part of a living tradition, which has been handed down willingly to my generation. Those who taught me believed that what they said was self-evident. I believe in my turn that it needs recording and handing on to the future. What he demands always works. And his notation is amazingly accurate.

Armed with a facsimile of the Folio, a simply edited but not-too-punctuated modern text, a glossary of archaic words and those that have changed their meaning, and an understanding of how Shakespeare guides his actors with his form, it is still possible to approach any of his texts with the confidence that they will be understood. Shakespeare's advice to the players is still potent.

BLANK VERSE

Shakespeare himself only uses the term 'blank verse' three times:

> **Hamlet** The lady shall say her mind freely, or the
> blank verse shall halt for it.

> **Jaques** (in AS YOU LIKE IT) Nay then, God b' wi'
> you an you talk in blank verse.

And **Benedick** (in MUCH ADO ABOUT NOTHING) when he speaks of running **'smoothly in the even road of a blank verse'**. 'Smoothness' seems to be a prerequisite of good verse speaking for Shakespeare: Hamlet also asks his actors to 'beget a smoothness'. The line presumably must be unbroken, not halting. Whenever Shakespeare speaks of blank verse, the need for smoothness seems to follow.

Shakespeare writes in blank verse using an unrhymed line of ten syllables, made up of five iambic feet:

di-DUM di-DUM di-DUM di-DUM di-DUM

This is a blank verse line – called blank because it doesn't rhyme with its adjacent lines. To Shakespeare, it represents the speech of everyday life. It is fleet, informative, and usually unpretentious. Its simplicity and directness make it paradoxically more transparent and colloquial than Shakespeare's prose. It is certainly more flexible. But then it is designed to be. An iambic measure, or foot, is 'di-Dum'. Five such feet make up an iambic pentameter. In ordinary English speech there are usually five beats or so to each spoken phrase. Perhaps that is why the common utterance of English verse and English dramatic poetry is a five-beat iambic line. French speech, by contrast, usually has six beats and that is the basic structure of the commonest French verse form – the Alexandrine. However complex in rhythm or clotted with imagery, the iambic lines of Shakespeare are never far away from the rhythms of ordinary English speech. This is why it can still sound so natural.

Take the lines that start THE TWO GENTLEMEN OF VERONA – a play which is one of Shakespeare's earliest, if not the earliest:

> **Cease to persuade, my loving Proteus.**
> **Home-keeping youths have ever homely wits.**

Shakespeare's prowess as a master of Elizabethan rhetoric is already impressive and can provoke a few scholarly terms to substantiate the claim. The two lines are regular

iambic pentameters that both begin with an **irregular inversion** called a **trochee**: **DUM-di** instead of **di-DUM**. Both lines are **end-stopped** and use **pun, antithesis, alliteration, oxymoron** and a highly developed use of **assonance**.

But let me rely less on the technical terms. They are enough to frighten anyone away from Shakespeare – especially young actors who value spontaneity, or readers who are made to feel inferior by academic jargon. Who cares? Why bother? What do all these archaic words have to do with the speaking of the lines or the necessary business of the play? How can they help? Well, these terms can be off-putting, but what they represent can still help us *understand* in the theatre or the study.

We must therefore demystify the old rhetorical terms and show them for what they are: highly practical tools that lead directly to some knowledge of what Shakespeare actually *heard* when he wrote the line. From them, we can deduce what formal shape (rhythm, emphasis, tempo) he was demanding. And all these clues teach us how to make the plays into public utterance, and finally how to act them.

Take the second line. It is a regular five-beat iambic line with an inversion, or trochee, on the first foot ('**Home**-keeping' instead of 'Home-**keeping**') to give emphasis to the word 'home'. There is a startling antithesis (the balance of opposites) between 'Home-keeping' and 'homely wits' and a pun or quibble on 'home' and 'homely'. If a young man stays at home instead of taking on the world, he will be 'homely' – that is domestic, unexceptional, even boring. There is an oxymoron (a flat contradiction between two opposites) between 'homely' and 'wit'. The young man is unlikely to be witty if he is homely; or homely if he is witty. He can't be both. And wit belongs to the world, and usually to the city. The stay-at-home will not have it.

These two lines give a complete philosophy of why the nest has to be vacated by the young. 'Wit' is knowledge, brain power, intellect (as well as plainly being smart). Homely wits are also not likely to get on in the world. There are many more clues buried in these two lines. And they all relate to wit – which I take to be an amusing or ironic phrase that illuminates by paradox or surprises by incongruity. It helps us to understand at the very moment that it entertains and challenges our understanding.

Once Shakespeare's clues have been listed, they can be applied with pleasure; and the actor or reader will know a great deal more about Shakespeare's intent. For a start, he will *hear* the play.

'YOU CAN'T IMPROVISE THIS SHIT...'

Years ago, I directed Dustin Hoffman as Shylock. He tried, great actor as he is, to get in touch with the character's feeling by improvisation. It is a common and valued technique among modern actors. To aid him, Dustin brandished one of those dismal editions that have Shakespeare's text on one side and an approximate (sometimes very approximate) modern English version on the page opposite. Assisted by this crib, he worked the scenes in modern speech. He tried to make Shakespeare meet the Method.

It was marvellous to watch because the improvisations were very alive. But they weren't Shakespeare. I was politely discouraging because I was entirely sceptical about where the exercise was leading. Dustin might create (indeed he rapidly did) a mesmerising modern Shylock, but he still had finally to come back to Shakespeare's text. Would this contemporary business man, delightfully Jewish and full of wit, ever want to say the words of Shakespeare, which are a fusion of the English Old Testament and colloquial Elizabethan speech? I didn't think so. While Dustin's improvisations might be helpful for charting his inner life, they would be of little help in speaking Shylock.

One morning, Dustin arrived looking haggard: he confessed that he had hardly slept at all. He had been working and worrying all night, picking out the clues I had given him, and trying to match them with his improvised speech. Then he had finally come to a conclusion. 'You can't improvise this shit,' he announced. I agreed: 'First comes the form and second comes the feeling,' I said, trying to keep the note of triumph out of my voice.

From now on, Dustin's whole attitude changed. He became a convert to Shakespeare's method. He worked assiduously on the form of the text, letting it guide him to the feelings and all the contradictions and complexities that he had to share with the audience. By the time we reached New York, he was speaking Shylock immaculately. At the same time, he *was* Shylock, apparently speaking spontaneously. There was nothing imposed, nothing abstract or mechanical about his speech. He was not repeating it, he was minting it at the moment he spoke it. It was always surprising because it was so tinglingly alive. It was *his*; yet most of all it was undoubtedly Shakespeare's.

Shakespeare's form then is made up of rhythm, rhyme, antithesis, personification, paradox and all the other ancient verbal techniques of the rhetorician. Actors may be able to make 'metaphor', 'irony' or 'simile' live; they may even be able to deal with 'blank verse', 'end-stopped lines' or 'iambic pentameters'. But when it comes to 'epistrophe' or 'epanalepsis' they may want to return to modern colloquial drama. But

Shakespeare's form helps us to know what he means. It works as well in a contemporary theatre as an ancient one; and it doesn't require radio mikes. Once the modern actor is secure in them, the rhetorical devices still support and inspire his emotional journey.

Shakespeare uses all the ancient techniques of rhetoric. He must have learned them at Stratford-upon-Avon Grammar School, where such matters would have been drilled into young scholars as an aid to writing and speaking Latin prose. Shakespeare's form, then, needs to be studied first. And this is the reverse of modern practice. The first question that the actor must ask about a speech is not who he is playing or what the character wants; first he must ask *what* the character says and *how* he says it.

In modern naturalistic drama, the feeling is often more important than the form. And unfortunately, a hundred years of Stanislavsky and the elaboration of his acting techniques into the American Method have resulted in many English-speaking actors believing that if they feel right, they will speak right. If the emotion is there, they trust that Shakespeare's blank verse or Tennessee Williams' long antithetical sentences, or Beckett's precise pauses will follow automatically. They don't. Shakespeare's text is a complex score that demands to be read as a piece of music, learned like the steps of a dance, or practised like the strokes of a duel. The form of the text is the end result; and when the actor fulfils its demands, he should be very near what Shakespeare heard. But by then, the actor should, like the singer with his notes, or the dancer with his steps, have made his feelings look spontaneous. He has 'made the speech his own' to quote the cliché used in all forms of performance art when the artist achieves freedom and appears to be inventing what he presents as he presents it.

Let me again stress that Shakespeare never tells the actor *how* he reaches these conclusions. And although the genius of Shakespeare is there to inspire the actor and so understand *why*, these motives are susceptible to an infinite number of interpretations and provide him with a multitude of choices. Out of them, he must make something credible to his audience.

I use the word 'credible' rather than 'true', because there is nothing true about standing on a stage and repeating someone else's words, disguised in a period costume, and simulating an emotion that is only partially being experienced. Yet if the actor is credible to his audience they will imagine what these circumstances would be like in reality. Meanwhile, the whole proceeding remains artificial. 'The truth is that the spectators are always in their senses and know, from the first act to the last, that the stage is only a stage and that the players are only players': Dr Johnson recognised that this dichotomy is part of the pleasure of theatre. We can lose ourselves in make-believe because we continue to know that it is only make-believe. If Titus Andronicus really cut off his hand, the audience would riot and the theatre would be closed.

THE MERCHANT OF VENICE, Peter Hall Company at the Phoenix Theatre 1989.
Geraldine James as Portia, Leigh Lawson as Antonio and Dustin Hoffman as Shylock.

To the great *Variety* of *Readers*.

Rom the moſt able,to him that can but ſpell: There you are number'd. We had rather you were weighd. Eſpecially, when the fate of all Bookes depends vp on your capacities : and not of your heads alone, but of your purſes. Well ! It is now publique, & you wil ſtand for your priuiledges wee know : to read, and cenſure. Do ſo,but buy it firſt. That doth beſt commend a Booke, the Stationer ſaies. Then, how odde ſoeuer your braines be, or your wiſedomes, make your licence the ſame,and ſpare not. Iudge your ſixe-pen'orth, your ſhillings worth, your fiue ſhillings worth at a time, or higher, ſo you riſe to the iuſt rates, and welcome. But, what euer you do, Buy. Cenſure will not driue a Trade, or make the Iacke go. And though you be a Magiſtrate of wit, and ſit on the Stage at *Black-Friers*, or the *Cock-pit*, to arraigne Playes dailie, know, theſe Playes haue had their triall alreadie, and ſtood out all Appeales ; and do now come forth quitted rather by a Decree of Court, then any purchas'd *Letters* of commendation.

It had bene a thing, wo confeſſe, worthie to haue bene wiſhed,that the Author himſelfe had liu'd to haue ſet forth, and ouerſeen his owne writings ; But ſince it hath bin ordain'd otherwiſe,and he by death departed from that right,we pray you do not envie his Friends,the office of their care, and paine, to haue collected & publiſh'd them ; and ſo to haue publiſh'd them, as where (before) you were abus'd with diuerſe ſtolne, and ſurreptitious copies, maimed,and deformed by the frauds and ſtealthes of iniurious impoſtors, that expos'd them : euen thoſe, are now offer'd to your view cur'd, and perfect of their limbes; and all the reſt, abſolute in their numbers, as he conceiued the. Who,as he was a happie imitator of Nature,was a moſt gentle expreſſer of it. His mind and hand went together: And what he thought, he vttered with that eaſineſſe, that wee haue ſcarſe receiued from him a blot in his papers. But it is not our prouince,who onely gather his works, and giue them you, to praiſe him. It is yours that reade him. And there we hope,to your diuers capacities, you will finde enough, both to draw, and hold you : for his wit can no more lie hid, then it could be loſt. Reade him, therefore ; and againe, and againe : And if then you doe not like him, ſurely you are in ſome manifeſt danger, not to vnderſtand him. And ſo we leaue you to other of his Friends, whom if you need,can bee your guides : if you neede them not, you can leade your ſelues,and others. And ſuch Readers we wiſh him.

Iohn Heminge.
Henrie Condell.

from the First Folio of Shakespeare's plays, 1623

THE TEXT

Shakespeare wrote (or collaborated on in a major way) some forty plays during twenty to twenty-five years. He therefore wrote about two plays a year. This is a large though not phenomenal number, especially by Elizabethan standards; but the range and variety of his work – from comedy through history to tragedy and romance – is unmatchable. Only half of his plays appeared in print while he lived, and though he saw his narrative poems (THE RAPE OF LUCRECE and VENUS AND ADONIS) through the press, there is no evidence that he was concerned directly with the publication of the single plays as Quartos. But then he was writing scripts for actors, not plays for readers.

The Quartos are a motley collection of good texts, bad texts, pirated texts and half-remembered texts. Our main source for Shakespeare is not them but the Folio of 1623. It contains thirty-seven of the plays and brings us as close to Shakespeare and his theatre as we can ever hope to get. The Folio was compiled by his two friends and fellow actors Heminge and Condell. Without their care and dedication, eighteen of the plays – MACBETH and ANTONY AND CLEOPATRA among them – would have been lost. The Folio is a record of what was said, but unfortunately not what was done, in the Elizabethan theatre four hundred years ago. Without it, we would know in every sense less about Shakespeare. But while the Folio, with its archaic and inconsistent lineation, brings us into the playhouse, there are very few stage directions which relate to the nature of the performance (Coriolanus' *'Holds her by the hand, silent'* is one of the very few). Those we have may be by Shakespeare or they may not. The Folio also poses all kinds of problems of mis-spellings, misprints and inaccuracies. With the help of computers, we think we know how many printers set the type of the Folio, and we also know something of these printers' individual tastes in spelling. But what was Shakespeare's own taste? Lost.

But then Shakespeare was not only a playwright; he was an actor and a major figure in the running of a theatre company. The number of plays mounted was necessarily prodigious; a run of half a dozen or so performances was a great success. Until Ben Jonson – who had scholarly pretensions and was much mocked for them – no dramatist thought of issuing his playscripts in a collected edition. Indeed it may well have been Ben Jonson who inspired Heminge and Condell to save Shakespeare for us. If he could have Collected Works, so could Shakespeare. The pressure and the activity at the playhouse must have been much like the great studio days in Hollywood in the 1930s. The dramatist would need to be thinking of his next play well before this one had its first performance. There was no time to conserve the work of the past. If it was successful, it was still alive in the heads of the actors; if it wasn't, it was quickly forgotten.

The purity of the Folio text, naïve though it can be, also reveals clues for the actor, who can, with practice, 'hear' the shape of the original play in a way that is impossible with the over-punctuated texts of later editors. They have been busy brushing up and correcting Shakespeare's grammar for centuries. Generally speaking, they punctuate for reading, not for speaking, so the actor must be wary.

Shakespeare, in spite of changes in vocabulary and a dependency on a system of rhetoric that is by now largely archaic, still communicates with astonishing clarity. Much of this clarity is the result of the focus that is given by the form. We listen to what is important, note what is provocative and yet have time to be stirred by complex and ambiguous images.

There can be no art without form. Form disciplines the inspiration and makes it expressive. Form contains the emotion and ensures that it is credible, and not indulgent. But the paradox of art is that the rules of form must always be challenged in order to achieve spontaneity. Yet they must not be completely destroyed. There is a balance between discipline and freedom which only the great creative genius or the astonishing performer can achieve.

Shakespeare and Mozart have a strange similarity as artists: they both used and abused what they inherited. Shakespeare received a formal tradition of English blank verse from Marlowe. Mozart inherited the shape and architectural symmetry of Baroque music. For Shakespeare, it was possible to take the regularity of the iambic pentameter, and, by contradicting it with irregularities and cross-rhythms which almost (but not quite) destroy the form, make an infinitely expressive means of conveying emotion. By the Late Plays, he is writing with a freedom that relies on knowing that his actors always have a regular iambic pentameter beating in their heads, like the pulse of a sophisticated jazz group. They can play *with* it or move *against* it in order to express emotion or tension, confusion or resolution.

The eighteenth century knew very well what music was and should be. Mozart's energy challenges this certainty. His sudden shifts of key, his chromaticisms, the contradiction that so many of his phrases offer to the accepted forms of the eighteenth century, not only point the way to Beethoven and the Romantics; they enable him to express heartbreak and pain in counterpoint to the balance and serenity of the classical world. He deepens music so that it takes on a tragic dimension. Shakespeare did the same with his words. The Elizabethans knew very well what iambic verse should be, and Shakespeare, in the interests of spontaneity, often comes near to destroying it. This produces a tension and therefore keeps the speech dramatic. Those who came after him – Tourneur, Webster and Middleton among them – went further and presided over the collapse of the tradition. Gradually, the iambics become prose – or something very near to it. The form is changed and is reliant on the balance of phrase against phrase rather than the established rhythm of the iambic line.

THE SANCTITY OF THE LINE

Faced with a comma, the modern actor loves to stop when he shouldn't; he loves to explore the pause, because he believes that pauses make a text sound spontaneous. But pauses destroy the basic energy and shape of the Shakespearean line: they do not make for *smoothness*. And Shakespeare's architecture in his verse is entirely dependent on the preservation of the iambic line. His form is destroyed by acting single words rather than lines. This may come from a wholly laudable desire to make the audience understand an archaic word. But it chops up the lines and loses the energy. The speech then does not 'trip on the tongue'; nor does it produce a performance that makes an audience run eagerly after it. Chopping up lines into little naturalistic gobbets may sound 'modern', but it plays hell with the meaning. And by chopping it up, the actors begin to communicate in irregular phrases rather than in the full iambic line. Consequently the actor becomes slower than the audience. The sanctity of the line is betrayed and Shakespeare's primary means of giving out information rapidly and holding our attention is destroyed.

Sadly, during the last twenty years, performances of Shakespeare have become slower and slower, and the running times of the plays longer and longer. Yet the plays have not generally been cut. They have lost energy by the use of an italicised delivery which makes the audience feel that they are being lectured. If the lines are spoken trippingly, the audience is alert; they have to be attentive. If individual words are over-emphasised, the energy is halted and the audience's attention flags.

A text with minimal punctuation based on meaning should be the basis of any theatre work. I have often found that a typescript stripped of everything but the essential full stops is the best beginning. Having established the text, what clues has Shakespeare left to guide the performer? They can all be revealed by studying the form of the writing. I will first attempt to set them down. Then I will analyse a series of speeches in chronological order from Shakespeare's beginnings as a dramatist to his last plays. This progress will recognise how Shakespeare's style changed as he moved towards maturity; but it will also demonstrate that he discarded nothing in his style that was useful. By the end, his verse is many-faceted; his styles and the styles of his company of actors fused into one of the most expressive ways of telling a story in public that man has ever invented. And he must have known, as his verse became freer and more irregular, that it was being spoken by actors who had an inner rhythm of the iambic line that they had lived and worked with for fifteen or twenty years.

Various types of prose will also feature in this survey. The clues in the prose are often quite different from the clues in the verse. I shall deal with the verse first and then, after a general consideration of the prose, illustrate those rhetorical devices which are common to both.

To Shakespeare, verse is to be spoken quickly and 'trippingly on the tongue' as the simulation of ordinary speech. Yet it is capable of elevation into metaphor in a split second. Prose is heavier and usually gives the antithetical analysis of the rational man – be he priest or lawyer or gravedigger. Indeed, while prose is frequently used to represent the speech of the common people, it is not usually colloquial at all. The constables and the shepherds often speak with the pretensions of the pedant. They possess the pompous anxiety of those who have not been schooled to speak 'properly'. Shakespeare is merciless when faced with pretension.

The clues in the text – both verse and prose – are part of an acting tradition that has nearly vanished. Since rhetoric and classical form are out of fashion, they are neglected both in the college and on the stage. Yet why should Shakespeare bother to write in verse if he meant the scrupulously constructed lines to be chopped up and their structure ignored?

VERSE

One of the problems of teaching actors verse is that the moment they have learned the rules, they can be confronted with a line where Shakespeare deliberately breaks them. One of the most famous lines in the English language is not a regular iambic pentameter:

To be or not to be that is the question

It actually contains a beat too many:

To BE or NOT to BE that IS the QUES-tion

The irregular extra syllable at the end of the line (known to grammarians, though it needn't worry us, as a 'feminine ending') frees the verse colloquially and makes Hamlet's question more urgent. It highlights the key word: 'Question'; and helps express the self-doubt, the insecurity. The actor who has just learnt the nature of an iambic line will find to his amazement that the next four lines continue the pattern of irregularity in Hamlet's speech. They *all* have a syllable too many.

> **To be or not to be that is the quest(ION)**
> **Whether tis nobler in the mind to suff(ER)**
> **The slings and arrows of outrageous for(TUNE)**
> **Or to take arms against a sea of troub(LES)**
> **And by opposing end them. To die to sleep…**

Only the last line is actually regular. All the rest have an additional syllable. As we shall see, the first task in approaching a speech is to make it scan, or find out why it doesn't. If there are extra syllables or irregularities, the actor must use them to express emotional turbulence, because that is what Shakespeare heard.

All the time, by inversions or by deliberate mis-scansions or by adding extra syllables which can only be scanned by eliding them, Shakespeare is preserving the tension between the colloquial nature of his verse and the regularity of the iambic beat. Again, it is like great jazz playing. It must never slip totally out of the rhythm, but it must challenge it all the time. It is dangerous, expressive and thus unexpected. Regular rhythms in verse become predictable and can sap an audience's attention. Shakespeare takes full account of this. There is an alertness in his use of irregularity. A film director tells his story and keeps our attention by changing shots, by *cutting* from one image to the next. Shakespeare uses irregularities in much the same way.

By his maturity, Shakespeare could risk a blank verse line which is a complete inversion of the normal rhythm, but which he knows will express the tragic agony of Lear. It is rhythmically the absolute opposite of what is expected:

NEVer. NEVer. NEVer. NEVer. NEVer.

It is not (which would be the correct scansion):

NeVER. NeVER. NeVER. NeVER. NeVER.

Shakespeare's irregularities only make emotional sense and can only affect an audience if the actor is riding on the underlying regularity beneath them. He must revel in the cross-rhythms, jump the irregularities and ride the bumps in scansion, in order to force the verse into shape. This tension to achieve regularity in the verse, in spite of all the irregularities, conveys the emotion, providing that the actor never gives up trying to make the line scan. He must always attempt to make the rough smooth. The nearer the verse gets to collapsing, the more tortured and emotional the expression. But it must never actually collapse; the excitement is that it often nearly does. The actor must risk rhythmical disintegration, yet never allow it to happen. What the audience receives is then dangerous and unpredictable.

To sum up: there are certainly an infinite number of ways of speaking a line of Shakespeare's wrongly. Any interpretation which breaks the line, unnecessarily distorts the iambic rhythm, ignores the antithesis, neglects the assonance, evades the alliteration or nine times out of ten does not lean on the end of the line (because that is where the primary meaning is usually found) will ruin the communication with the audience and what the actor is supposed to tell them by speaking the text.

But there is conversely no one correct way of speaking the line. There are always infinite choices for the actor provided the form is maintained. He is not bound by some rigid system – say rather that he is freed by a form which gives him infinite emotional possibilities. By observing the form, the actor's speech at its best sounds completely natural. The blank verse is made to sound like colloquial speech.

THE STRUCTURE OF THE LINE

Shakespeare's verse is entirely built on its linear structure. The iambic beat of the lines, their need to answer each other, the irregularities that stand out as emotional outbreaks, the care with which half-line meets with another half-line to make a whole – all these make a shape which is flexible yet consistent. But the sanctity of the line is paramount. It must be maintained wherever possible. The actor must therefore try to make every line scan; then the overriding tension between the regular pattern of the ideal verse line and what Shakespeare (in his quest for spontaneity and naturalness) wrote will keep the text alive.

Shakespeare's early plays have regular verse which is termed 'end-stopped'. This means more often than not that the sense and the punctuation point meet together at the end of each line. A line that runs on (called an **enjambment**) and stops in the middle of the next line with a full stop or a semi-colon (called the **caesura**) is a rarity. The extra syllable (the **feminine ending**) is also uncommon. **Pauses** – where half a line is omitted – are hardly used. The form of, for example, the HENRY VI plays is near-ritualistic, with regular linear verse that is often incantatory. The constant end-stopping risks monotony. Yet Shakespeare is already using the balance of one line with the next and the rhetorical effect of contrasts – particularly that of antithesis (which is contrasting ideas expressed by a parallelism of words which have strongly contrasting meanings):

> **Was never subject longed to be a King**
> **As I do long and wish to be a subject.**

Most of Shakespeare's verse, early and late, is weighted at the end of the iambic line. Seventy per cent of his verse has the crux – or the important meaning – in the last words of the line. To drop the end of the line (or to allow it to droop in the depressed inflections of modern Estuary English) usually produces a line with little meaning and no impact.

The end of each line is in fact a punctuation often more crucial than the regular punctuation itself. Unless it is observed, the audience is given too much information and is unable to take it in. For this reason, the end of the line must be lightly marked, rather as a pianist uses the legato pedal to shape the end of one phrase and announce the beginning of the next. It is unfortunate that in rhetorical terms it should be known as end-stopping, because there should, whenever possible, be no stop. It is rather a going-on point, an energetic hesitation that summons up the strength to proceed and define the next line. It does not stop, it energises. The actor hesitates in order to go on.

In my experience, there is always a natural inflection that each actor can find which phrases the line and marks its end, however lightly. It is of course permissible to slow up or accelerate on the line as part of a natural human inflection. But it is not possible to stop or fracture the line unless it is clearly the beginning of a marked pause. In this case, half the line will be missing.

Every great Shakespearean actor develops a way of expressing and endorsing the linear structure. In order to phrase naturally, there is an absolute need to *feel* where the end of the verse line occurs. To run the lines together risks incoherence and often necessitates a pause in the middle of the next line for breath or for sense. This wrecks the structure of the verse. Laurence Olivier took nearly twenty years before he began to ride on the lines like an expert skier. Peggy Ashcroft marked the lines by accenting the last word, like a bell chiming; John Gielgud marked them by braying slightly on the last word. Ralph Richardson insisted on an upward inflection to sustain the line. All these great actors were responding to Shakespeare's linear needs and were insistent that the actor must always know where the end of the line occurs. This is not only the place where the primary meaning is expressed; it is the herald of the next complex thought. And it is always the place to breathe.

To sum up
The Structure of the Line

- *Try to make every line scan.*
- *Learn the end of the line.*
- *Work out a breathing pattern so that you always have breath in reserve.*
- *Breaths whether small or substantial should only be taken at the end of the line.*
- *Keep the line whole and play lines rather than words.*

SCANSION

The actor must always start by scanning the speech. 'Scanning' means trying to fit the five foot iambic rhythm to the given words.

If music be the food of love play on

is a perfectly regular blank verse line, colloquial, clear and proposing a richly mixed metaphor about appetite:

If MUSic BE the FOOD of LOVE play ON

Yet:

I know a bank where the wild thyme blows

is a seemingly regular iambic line which is in fact not regular at all. There is an inversion at the beginning of the line which colloquially would encourage an equal emphasis on the two words: '**I know**' instead of the correct scansion ' **I KNOW**' which sounds false. If regularity is to be observed, the accent will fall improbably on 'the', and if this is observed, the rhythm of the rest of the line collapses. The solution is to elide 'where the' so both words are off the beat. Then 'WILD THYME BLOWS' all have the possibility of a regular accent on each word. So we end up with:

I know a BANK where the WILD THYME BLOWS.

There are five beats but they are subtly distributed to herald a magical invocation. And the expectation in the line is utterly dependent on the counterpoint between the expected regularity and this hypnotic irregularity.

The tension between the regular and the irregular is one of Shakespeare's constant techniques. The first scanning is crucial: every line that is irregular or that contains an inversion, or has too few or too many syllables, needs to be registered and pondered over. A strong attempt must be made to make every line scan. The syllables must be counted and the variations from the norm of ten noted. Often the line can be made to scan by adopting an elision, like the 'where the' in Oberon's speech. But if irregularities remain after the elisions, there are usually emotional reasons for them. They have to be endorsed, because they are the signs of unrest in the character. And this unrest is always expressed in counterpoint to the regular pulse:

Leontes   Fie, fie, no thought of him.
The very thought of my revenges that way

Recoil upon me. In himself too mighty,
And in his parties, his alliance. Let him be
Until a time may serve. For present vengeance,
Take it on her. Camillo and Polixenes
Laugh at me, make their pastime at my sorrow.
They should not laugh if I could reach them, nor
Shall she, within my power.
(THE WINTER'S TALE, Act 2 Scene 3)

The scansion often guides us to the inflection:

Volumnia   For HOW can WE

Alas how CAN we for our country pray?
(CORIOLANUS, Act 5 Scene 3)

Volumnia's accent on the second 'can' shows the urgency of her plea.

By the time Shakespeare is in his maturity (the period of the great tragedies and the late plays), he has an unrivalled freedom in verse. Leontes' twisted passion is almost clinically expressed by his clotted, irregular rhythms and the lines that are packed with too many syllables as his tension mounts.

To sum up
Scansion

- *Try to make every line scan.*
- *See if anything can be elided in the interests of scansion.*
- *Let the five beats dictate the inflection if it sounds natural.*
- *Finally, the rhythm of the iambics should be lightly stated and as flexible as colloquial speech.*

THE CAESURA

Duke Our haste from hence is of so quick condition
That it prefers itself and leaves unquestioned
MATTERS OF NEEDFUL VALUE. WE SHALL WRITE TO YOU
As time and our concernings shall importune,
How it goes with us and do look to know
WHAT DOTH BEFALL YOU HERE. SO FARE YOU WELL.
To th' hopeful execution do I leave you
OF YOUR COMMISSIONS.
    Angelo   YET GIVE LEAVE, MY LORD,
That we may bring you something on the way.
(MEASURE FOR MEASURE, Act 1 Scene 1)

The half lines marked with capitals contain caesuras – a break in the middle of a line, frequently marked with a full stop or a semi-colon. It is usually a sense-break that invites the stop in mid-line and it follows a run-on. But the stop must not be so long that the whole line disintegrates. And it must be earned by a slow enough tempo on the first half of the line so that the slight pause can be taken without the disruption of the whole line. Again, the sanctity of the line must be preserved.

It is also essential that the two half-lines, whether they be internally within one character's speech (as in the first two examples here) or shared between two actors (as in the third example) make up a whole line which has the same pace, dynamic, rhythm and volume. The two half-lines thus make a whole, *although the dramatic motive of each half may be, and often is, entirely different*. The necessary change of pace required to earn the full stop occurs on the first half of the line and has an even more important purpose.

The caesura is in fact the means by which Shakespeare varies the tempo and orchestrates his verse. The first half of the caesura line usually slows things up so there is time for the sense-break. It is often more emotional or emphatic than what has gone before. It is certainly always significant. Modern actors and directors are taught to divide the dialogue of a scene into 'beats' or 'paragraphs of emotional action'. A different objective or a different need creates a different mood. And this gives variety of tone and pace. But Shakespeare tells us where the beats change *before* we begin rehearsal by using the caesura as a means of altering the mood and tempo of the first half of the line in order to earn the slight pause of the sense-break. A complete iambic line that ends with a full stop can also of course provide the opportunity for a new beat. But it is not mandatory. The break at the half-line caesura always is.

Technically, in order to preserve the structure of the whole line, the tempo, dynamic, volume of the two half-lines must again be the same. Two half lines make one **smooth** whole.

Shakespeare's text is peppered with half-lines of this kind. They always indicate a fundamental change of pace and attitude where they are shared between actors, and they are of great assistance in persuading them to play together, to be sensitive to each other's tone. At a moment like this the actors have to help each other. The first 'feeds'; and when the second responds, the line is complete.

There are a multitude of half-lines in Shakespeare. This exchange is in JULIUS CAESAR:

> **Peace count the clock.**
> > **The clock hath stricken three.**

Obviously the second actor comes in on cue: that is why there are two half-lines. The two actors together have to make one line out of the two. The mood and motive of each character is completely different and they can show that while still not disrupting the line. But where does the clock strike? The normal way of playing these two half-lines is:

> **(Bell.)**
> **Peace count the clock. (Bell. Pause. Bell. Pause.)**
> > **The clock hath stricken three.**

This is not only predictable (and thus undramatic), it also takes a great deal of time. It puts a pause within the line which Shakespeare specifically did not intend. If he had meant it, he would have written it. He very carefully did the opposite and made the two half-lines into one.

This is what is written. The bell interrupts the speech of Trebonius.

> **Trebonius** **There is no fear in him, let him not die,**
> > **For he will live and laugh at this hereafter. (Bell. Bell. Bell.)**
> **Brutus** **Peace count the clock.**
> **Cassius** > **The clock hath stricken three.**

Brutus' line is in a slow tempo, cautious, haunted. He has heard the first two strokes of the bell and the third comes as he begins his line. Against the silence of the bell after it has finished its three strokes, the line is completed in a similarly haunted tone by Cassius. All this produces a chilling moment. The conspirators know that the hour of the assassination of Caesar comes with the dawn. None of them is eager for this night to hurry away. But the dawn is getting near and Cassius knows it. Shakespeare's rhythms show this fear and they are entirely unexpected. His sense of timing is never ours.

To sum up
The Caesura

- *The caesura is the break in mid-line marked with a full stop or a semi-colon. It follows an end-of-line when the sense runs on, but usually as a qualification or a climax.*
- *Learn from the beginning when the caesuras occur.*
- *Consider what emotional change is necessary on the first half of the caesura line in order to earn the time for a full stop or sense-break.*
- *The sanctity of the line means that sense-break can only happen if the tempo of the whole line is slow enough.*
- *Never pause in mid-line if the sense runs on, and only pause in mid-line if the caesura has dictated it.*
- *Notice that the half-lines either side of a caesura are often emotionally very rich. This is another reason for taking time.*
- *The two halves of the line must make one in tempo, dynamic and volume, even though the emotions are usually different.*
- *When two characters each have a half-line that makes up one line, the second character must come in precisely on cue and the tempo and dynamic of the two halves must make one line. Smoothness is the objective.*

MONOSYLLABLES

On any page of Shakespeare's, of whatever period, twenty-five per cent of the lines are made up of monosyllables. What does that signify? Shakespeare was probably hardly aware that he was writing in monosyllables; but he undoubtedly heard the line in a specific way. Consider the absolutely regular, monosyllabic iambic pentameter that begins THE MERCHANT OF VENICE:

In sooth I know not why I am so sad

Monosyllabic lines are an important guide to tempo and to emphasis; and they are a major help to the actor in the early stages of his work on a speech. This line contains three very conscious sibilances: 'sooth', 'so', 'sad'. But the most noticeable fact is if we try to speak this iambic line quickly and trippingly, if we hurry it, it becomes incomprehensible. It also has no rhythm.

InsoothIknownotwhyIamsosad

And so the actor has learnt a startling clue: monosyllables always indicate a slowing up, or a spreading of the speech. Otherwise the line is incomprehensible. Slowed up it scans, easily:

In sooth I know not why I am so sad

Again it is the actor's task to find out *why* the line is slow, and what emotions he must engender in himself to produce these measured accents. But slow it always is and always must be, otherwise Antonio makes no sense. In addition, there is of course a subtext here: Antonio knows very well why he is feeling sad, both professionally and personally, and these weighty monosyllables release the subtext, and intrigue the audience in this first moment of the play. Why is he sad? What is his secret? We must find out…

Shakespeare's form again imposes a discipline – it is based on the sanctity of the line. So whatever else is done, the rhythm of the line must be preserved. To put in pauses and breaks –

In sooth (big pause) I know not WHY (hesitation) I am so (pause) SAD

– ruins the form, even if it makes the actor feel modern and colloquial. Antonio's frustrations – what he is hiding and the cause of his anxieties – must be expressed by due accent and emphasis. But the line must still hold its iambic purity. It must be smooth.

An actor can often be led to the interpretation of a line by looking at the form, particularly when the line is monosyllabic. But recently I heard an Othello bellow his great monosyllabic line:

Keep up your bright swords for the dew will rust them.

The noise stopped the riot, but the line was too fast to be comprehensible. It was so frantic that it gave no impression of the strong naïvity of this character, so certain of his authority.

Let us dissect the line. First of all it is monosyllabic, so it is measured; it cannot be snatched or hurried. Othello's entrance, not his line, stills the crowd, and the previous, hurried, half-iambic shouts of the brawl are silenced. Then comes the line. We are ready for a full iambic pentameter to resolve the chaos. It must be slow enough though for Othello to *think* the image and for the audience to appreciate the wry wit of bright swords being rusted by dew. The inversion of the iambic rhythm at the beginning of the line, and the feminine ending give it a natural colloquial ease and provide a strong accent on 'rust'. This dew has hyperbolical powers and this is a man diffusing an ugly situation by wit. It is also an actor economically establishing his character. There is nothing rough or rude about this Moor.

CYMBELINE, one of the Late Plays, displays a mastery of verse which is almost symphonic. The young princes who have been brought up in the wilderness, Guiderius and Arviragus, have a directness and simplicity which is often monosyllabic. It contrasts markedly with the more image-laden speech of their mentor, Belarius. But the Princes' directness allows for the sharp focus of individual words:

> **What should we speak of**
> **When we are old as you? When we shall hear**
> **The rain and wind beat dark December, how,**
> **In this our pinching cave, shall we discourse**
> **The freezing hours away?**
> (CYMBELINE, Act 3 Scene 3)

The monosyllables give a certain gravitas to what is being said. The antithesis between 'speak' and 'hear' delivers through a series of monosyllables the alliterative 'dark December' and the multi-syllable word, ominous and climactic. The end of each line sets up the next. Arviragus is trying to define – to express his thoughts in clear terms.

Monosyllables allied with the changes of tone on the caesuras go a long way to orchestrating and defining the shape of any speech of Shakespeare's.

To sum up
Monosyllables

- *Recognise the monosyllabic lines.*
- *Isolate their more slow and measured tempi so that they are comprehensible.*
- *Find an emotion that justifies the tempo.*

PAUSES

Pauses become more common as the verse becomes more complex. Timon and Leontes, even Prospero, are often so neurotic that they speak by fits and starts. Their pauses are written in quite clearly by the omission of two or three stresses ('feet' of the iambic line), rather than by punctuation. Clearly the breaking of the rules was becoming more and more Shakespeare's way of creating theatrical life.

The written-in pauses should of course be observed and an emotional justification found for them. But pauses should not be generally taken in the middle of full lines. It is possible to have a sense-break in the middle of a line at a caesura. But this must be earned, usually by slowing up the first half of the line. There is never justification for breaking a line with a pause when the sense continues.

The late plays contain more written-in pauses and there may be a reason for this. Pauses don't work well in large theatres in daylight. There is a lack of focus and a tendency (that must have been evident at the Globe) for spectators to feel that nothing is going on if no-one is speaking. This would not be so at the Blackfriars, the private indoor candlelit theatre where attention was easier to capture and pauses could be eloquently held.

Normally, Shakespeare is intent on preserving the pulse of his iambic lines and making the linear structure clear. To repeat an absolute: Shakespeare deals not in individual words, or in isolated phrases, but in complete lines. This is the norm which is the couterpoint to his frequent irregularities.

It is sometimes difficult to see from the text where a defined and written pause should be taken. It is usually after the half-line and is defined by missing feet. But the actor should always consider if the pause plays better before the half-line or after it. It is again a matter of actor's choice. Take Hamlet and Horatio in Act 5:

Hamlet   Let us know
            Our indiscretion sometimes serves us well
            When our dear plots do pall, and that should teach us
            There's a divinity that shapes our ends,
            Rough-hew them how we will.
Horatio That is most certain.
Hamlet Up from my cabin
            My sea-gown scarfed about me, in the dark…

Horatio can come in to complete Hamlet's line or he can pause, allowing the thought of the divinity that shapes our ends, to give a moment of reflection. Or Hamlet can pause after Horatio's line to let the moment sink in before beginning his malevolent tale of revenge. What is certain is that we have three incomplete lines that make up one complete line, a pause and a half-line. How the passage is phrased is up to the actors and the director. But it is mandatory to have a pause somewhere. Shakespeare wrote it.

There is another fascinating moment in the same scene where the pause is more clearly marked. Hamlet says, having described how he sent Rosencrantz and Guildenstern to their deaths:

> **Hamlet**   **Now the next day**
> **Was our sea-fight; and what to this was sequent**
> **Thou know'st already.** [*half-line missing*]
> **Horatio So Guildenstern and Rosencrantz go to't.**

The pause is clearly marked. Horatio is stunned by the vindictive relish with which Hamlet has told the story. So there is a stunned pause, followed by a rather lame colloquial line. He pretends he is not appalled.

To sum up
The Pause

- *Define where and how the pause is indicated.*
- *Note where Shakespeare has written the pause by the omission of two or three iambic accents.*
- *Never pause in the middle of a line if the sense continues.*
- *A sense-break can occur at the caesura if it can be earned by the slow tempo of the whole line.*
- *The actor must always know what his emotional journey is during a pause.*
- *A pause can always be taken at the end of a full line if emotionally it can be justified.*

RHYME

We think of rhyme as something primitive and naïve – the stuff of children's fables and nursery rhymes. For us, it has gone out of fashion. Actors, accordingly, faced with rhyming couplets, do their best to ignore them. But for the texture of Shakespeare's speech to be fully revealed, rhyme needs understanding and using as much as any other rhetorical device. It provides a verbal definition which is used in many different ways.

First, as Boyet's speech in Act 5 of LOVE'S LABOUR'S LOST reminds us, it gives a clear focus to plain narrative.

> **Boyet** Under the cool shade of a sycamore
> I thought to close mine eyes some half an **hour.**
> When lo, to interrupt my purposed **rest**
> Toward that shade I might behold **addressed**
> The King and his companions. **Warily**
> I stole into a neighbour thicket **by**
> And overheard what you shall **overhear:**
> That by and by disguised they will be **here.**

The whole passage captures the attention and fills the listeners with expectation. In addition to the rhyme, notice the change of pace on the caesura line.

> The King and his companions. Warily…

There is obviously a slow-up on the first half of the line in order to project the hushed surprise of seeing the King and his young companions. This slowness leads us into 'Warily' which is an end-of-line set-up for what happens next. It too is hushed. There are two half-rhymes here – 'sycamore' and 'hour'; 'warily' and 'by'. They should be relished and pointed up. They are part of the character's exuberance.

Particularly in the early plays, Shakespeare uses rhyme as a means of achieving wit. Berowne's speech in LOVE'S LABOUR'S LOST (Act 5 Scene 2) is a perfect example of the energy and delight that rhyme can bring:

> **Berowne** I see the trick on't. Here was a **consent,**
> Knowing aforehand of our **merriment,**
> To dash it like a Christmas **comedy.**
> Some carry-tale, some please-man, some slight **zany,**

> Some mumble-news, some trencher-knight, some Dick
> That smiles his cheek in years, and knows the trick
> To make my lady laugh when she's disposed,
> Told our intents before, which once disclosed,
> The ladies did change favours, and then we,
> Following the signs, wooed but the sign of she.

Rhyme is also used for setting scenes and provoking pictures in the audience's imagination, as in ROMEO AND JULIET, Act 2 Scene 2:

> The grey-eyed morn smiles on the frowning night
> Chequ'ring the eastern clouds with streaks of light.

There are also tonal points that call for rhymes. Shakespeare is keen throughout his career to finish a scene with the firm major chord that a rhyme provides:

> **Oberon** And look thou meet me ere the first cock crow.
> **Puck** Fear not, my lord, your servant shall do so.

Often the scene ends with a rhyme which not only rounds it off but promises the coming action like a trailer. Take this extract from HAMLET:

> **Hamlet**   The play's the thing
> Wherein I'll catch the conscience of the King.

Sometimes a scene – for example in MEASURE FOR MEASURE – ends not with an affirmation, but with a hideous doubt. This is also expressed in rhyme:

> **Angelo** Alack, when once our grace we have forgot
> Nothing goes right; we would and we would not.

Shakespeare is very fond of using archaic words and archaic verse forms to set up a different atmosphere. So Prospero's Epilogue is couched in four-beat (not five-beat) lines with rhymes that may remind us of medieval folk drama.

> **Prospero** Now my charms are all o'erthrown,
> And what strength I have's mine own,
> Which is most faint. Now 'tis true

> I must be here confined by you
> Or sent to Naples. Let me not,
> Since I have my dukedom got
> And pardoned the deceiver, dwell
> In this bare island by your spell;
> But release me from my bands
> With the help of your good hands.

Rhyme is also used in a black and humorous way. There is a grimness about Macbeth's couplet

> Hear it not, Duncan, for it is a knell
> That summons thee to heaven or to hell

which is both humorous and terrifying. Strangely enough, if the couplet is played absolutely straight, it has a Christmas card quality which is comical in the wrong way. With a touch of mordant humour, it sends shivers up the spine. The rhyme enhances this. All these considerations help the actor, because rhyme is always there to be used, not ignored. The character, as much as the actor, must invent the need for rhyme and fulfil it with an example he can relish. Rhyme should never be thrown away or shyly ignored.

In Shakespeare's hands, rhyme is a source of endless variety. When Romeo sees Juliet on the balcony, his need to describe her eyes leads him to rhyme:

> **Romeo** What if her eyes were there, they in her head,
> The brightness of her cheek would shame those stars
> As daylight doth a lamp; her eye in heaven
> Would through the airy region stream so **bright**
> That birds would sing and think it were not **night**.

To sum up
Rhyme

- *It is a punctuation.*
- *It can provoke a laugh.*
- *It can confirm a point either by comedy or a chilling seriousness.*
- *It can end a scene.*
- *It can add to wit and delight.*
- *Above all it must be used and enjoyed.*

PROSE

Where the verse trips along and is dependent on a sense of line, the prose demands specific pointing. On the surface, Shakespeare's prose is easier to speak than his verse. But the actor will mislead himself if he thinks of the prose as a more 'natural' representation of ordinary speech. The opposite is true. There is always a formality about Shakespeare's prose, a balance which springs initially from the character who is speaking it. Prose is about high seriousness, and it is often comic as a consequence. It may be the grandeur of the conceited Don Armado in LOVE'S LABOUR'S LOST, or the pretension of the ill-educated (such as Dogberry in MUCH ADO ABOUT NOTHING). But in either case it is shaped and formed in a very different way from the verse. The similarities are a number of rhetorical devices and those analysed from now on are common to both verse and prose.

There are some simple rules for the actor approaching a prose speech in Shakespeare:

- *Try to phrase to the end of the sentence and keep going to the full stop.*
- *Only breathe on the full stop.*
- *Emphasise and enjoy the balance of the antitheses, the chiming sounds of the alliterations and assonances, the power of the puns, the wit of the quibbles. Try to invent them.*
- *Go slowly enough for the shape and formality of the prose to be evident to the hearer. It should be slower and more didactic than the verse.*
- *Remember this is not natural speech; nor is it the simulation of natural speech. It is avowedly artificial.*

And this is the main point. There is always a deliberate formality about the prose; it is more self-conscious than the verse. Whereas the verse represents ordinary speech, the prose stands for heightened speech, whether pompous or pretentious or plainly serious. Perhaps the most self-conscious use of prose on a serious level in the plays is the oration that Brutus makes in JULIUS CAESAR (considered later in the Analytical Notes). The aesthetic discipline of this speech makes the freedom of Mark Antony's subsequent verse speech seem candid, informal and humane.

Prose is also the instrument of comedy because it oftens expresses the wrong-headed verbosity of a Bottom or a Dogberry as they strive to express themselves in educated speech which they do not naturally possess. Even the Gravediggers in HAMLET discourse like disputatious lawyers. The Lawyer, the Scholar, the Priest, as well as the Gravedigger, the Constable or the common recruit, all give themselves authority by prose.

The prose is held together by its balance of phrase on phrase and thought on thought: either they dispute or they conform; they may affirm or they may deny. The pointing of the individual words is usually marked by alliteration. And these are the words to emphasise – to be stressed lightly and wittily.

Close study usually reveals that there is much more alliteration than we think in even the best known prose speeches:

> sPeak the sPeech I Pray you as I Pronounced it to
> you – TriPPingly on the Tongue; but if you Mouth
> it as Many of your Players do, I had as Lief the
> Town crier had spoke my Lines.

Alliteration binds the sentences together.

After all the analysis, Shakespeare's verse plays quickly because in each line there are finally only two or three words which are important. They can be leapt on like a series of stepping stones. The prose is more measured and a sense of balance means that phrase answers phrase and word chimes with word. There are many more emphatic words than there are in the verse.

Shakespeare is always very sensitive about moving from prose into verse and back again. The actor has to be equally sensitive to the emotional developments in the scene which these rhythmic changes illustrate.

In the second act of ANTONY AND CLEOPATRA, Antony and Enobarbus have just arrived from Egypt and there is a scene of hot political debate in verse between Antony, Caesar and Lepidus. With their exit, Enobarbus, Agrippa and Maecenas are left on the stage. The temperature drops, as they speak prose. But within twenty lines, they are back into verse again, so that the rough, tough soldier, Enobarbus, can wax emotional about Cleopatra – the last character the audience would expect to be so affected. The transition is effected by a half-line made up of two trochees, a stressed syllable followed by a short syllable. The transition is breathtaking. The rhythm delivers the verse.

> **Maecenas** She's a most triumphant lady if report be square to her.
> **Enobarbus** When she first met Mark Antony, she pursed up his
> heart upon the river of Cydnus.

> **Agrippa** There she appeared indeed, or my reporter devised
> well for her.
> **Enobarbus** I will tell you.
> The barge she sat in, like a burnished throne,
> Burned on the water.

The last two and a half lines achieve iambic verse. Shakespeare becomes adept at moving from verse to prose and then back to verse again. The shift to verse usually – as here – heralds a higher emotional temperature.

In TWELFTH NIGHT, when Olivia falls in love with Viola in front of our eyes (to be analysed later), Shakespeare uses each transition back into verse to lift the emotional stakes. The prose asserts the rational and often deflates the emotion; the verse defines the lyrical and the passionate. Yet at times, when prose and verse are mixed, the prose takes on an almost iambic pulse as it hands on the sense to the verse.

The first scene of TROILUS AND CRESSIDA illustrates this point. Troilus speaks verse, Pandarus prose.

> **Troilus** The Greeks are strong, and skilful to their strength,
> Fierce to their skill, and to their fierceness valiant.
> But I am weaker than a woman's tear,
> Tamer than sleep, fonder than ignorance,
> Less valiant than the virgin in the night,
> And skilless as unpractised infancy.
> **Pandarus** Well, I have told you enough of this. For my part, I'll
> not meddle nor make no farther. He that will have a
> cake out of the wheat must tarry the grinding.
> **Troilus** Have I not tarried?
> **Pandarus** Ay, the grinding; but you must tarry the boulting.
> **Troilus** Have I not tarried?
> **Pandarus** Ay, the boulting; but you must tarry the leavening.
> **Troilus** Still have I tarried?
> **Pandarus** Ay, to the leavening; but here's yet in the word
> 'hereafter' the kneading, the making of the cake, the
> heating of the oven, and the baking – nay, you must
> stay the cooling too, or ye may chance burn your lips.
> **Troilus** Patience herself, what goddess e'er she be,
> Doth lesser blench at suff'rance than I do.

Troilus speaks emphatically in iambics. Pandarus undercuts with his own anarchic prose rhythms. The speech patterns here absolutely reveal the characters: Troilus is naïve, resolute, firm, candid; Pandarus manipulative, mocking, complaining. If the two actors preserve their rhythms as if they were in a contest with each other, the scene almost plays itself.

To sum up
Prose

- *The prose is formal, antithetical and slower than the verse.*
- *The meaning needs careful unpicking and telling with the rational care of a lawyer making his case.*
  Relish the paradoxes, the quibbles, the contradictions.
- *The prose loves contradictions and so should the character.*
- *Technically, only breathe on the full stop – then it is possible to shape the frequently long sentences.*

RHETORICAL DEVICES
FIGURES OF SPEECH COMMON TO VERSE AND PROSE

The primary task of the Shakespearean actor is to observe the form, mint the images, relish the rhymes, and consciously deliver an explanation of himself in words. That is why the actor needs to appreciate the components of rhetoric. The following figures of speech are common to both verse and prose. Acting Shakespeare is a matter of endorsing them.

Metaphor and Simile

Shakespeare's dialogue, whether verse or prose, can move from plain speech to complex metaphor and back again with the greatest ease. Shakespeare loves mixed metaphors – a habit which drove grammarians and the French classicists mad for centuries. A metaphor is a figure of speech in which a word or phrase is transferred to another object or action (so it can be different from it, or analogous to it), which is illuminated by the comparison. MACBETH is rich in metaphor because it deals with the fevered images of a murderer who is cursed with an imagination. It has conveniently supplied all the examples needed for this section. When Macbeth hears of the death of Banquo and the escape of his son Fleance, he says

> **Thanks for that.**
> **There the grown serpent lies. The worm that's fled**
> **Hath nature that in time will venom breed,**
> **No teeth for th' present.**

The metaphors are so blindingly surreal that we don't question that a great warrior could have an imagination hot enough to invent them. Here the grown serpent, the dead body of Banquo, lies dead in its moment of full-growth. The worm has fled – Fleance who will grow into something venomous and dangerous with teeth to kill. For the moment, the boy is no risk, but he is a mortal threat in the future.

Simile is a figure of speech involving the comparison of one thing with another, often cued by 'as' or 'like', and it is as common as the use of metaphor. The comparison or resemblance illuminates the meaning:

> **Then comes my fit again; I had else been perfect,**
> **Whole as the marble, founded as the rock,**
> **As broad and general as the casing air…**

But now we move from simile to metaphor:

> But now I am cabined, cribbed, confined, bound in
> To saucy doubts and fears.

Often Shakespeare moves into more impressionistic images, as in Macbeth's

> And pity, like a naked new-born babe,
> Striding the blast, or heaven's cherubin, horsed
> Upon the sightless couriers of the air,
> Shall blow the horrid deed in every eye
> That tears shall drown the wind...

Pity is personified, vulnerable as a new-born babe. It's still capable of survival because it can stride through the storm and survive it. The image now develops: the news of the murder will fill the heavens, and there will be universal grief and tears in every eye. Under the pressure of guilt, the simile develops into an apocalyptic vision. Finally the tears of all humanity will drown the wind; the hyperbole takes in the universe and all mankind.

This speech develops into a miraculous transformation of ambition as a personified metaphor:

> I have no spur
> To prick the sides of my intent, but only
> Vaulting ambition which o'erleaps itself
> And falls on th'other.

Several interpretations of the metaphor are possible here. Ambition always over-achieves, always leaps beyond itself and tries to destroy the competition – and risks destroying itself. But there is also the banality of Ambition vaulting into the saddle and falling off the other side of the horse. Shakespeare is always adept at yoking the commonplace to the metaphysical.

The actor's use of metaphor and simile must always be conscious because the character's use of it is conscious. A sense of invention is needed to define for the audience the emotions the character is experiencing. Metaphor and simile obviously inspire the actor to an understanding of the character; but it is by the *minting* of the images that the character tells the tale of his emotions.

Antithesis

This is one of Shakespeare's commonest devices, repeatedly used in order to maintain the lucidity of the text. It shows the actor which words to point and what emotional base he needs in order to make the comparisons credible:

> Age cannot wither her, nor custom stale
> Her infinite variety

This is Enobarbus on Cleopatra. 'Age' is balanced with 'custom', and 'wither' as a verb with 'stale'. The paradox is eloquent and needs pointing. Note also that antitheses often find humour in the comparison – ranging from the delightful to the grotesque. 'Stale', for instance, is an Elizabethan word that describes the contents of the privy.

Alliteration

Alliteration is the use of a series of words which start with the same group of consonants. It was the versification which made up the bones of old and middle English, drama and poetry. But it was much used and appreciated by Shakespeare because it is an attention-getter, particularly in the open air.

The actor must not be shy of alliteration. Yet he must lean on the common consonants with discretion. The alliterated words are the words that need pointing, as three examples from A MIDSUMMER NIGHT'S DREAM demonstrate. First Titania's graphic description of the mother of the beloved Indian child who would sit with her:

> When we have laughed to see the Sails conCeive
> And grow Big-Bellied With the Wanton Wind...

Shakespeare also uses alliteration in order to mock the amateur dramatics of Bottom and his friends and perhaps point out that the device needs to be used discreetly. He seems almost to be parodying his own style in ROMEO AND JULIET. Pyramus laments the death of his Thisbe and it is very close to the lamentations of the Capulet family over Juliet.

> Which is – no, no, which was – the fairest dame
> That Lived, that Loved, that Liked, that Looked, with cheer.
> Come tears Confound;
> Out sword and wound
> The Pap of Pyramus...

And an excellent prose example comes at the moment when Bottom wakes up in the wood and calls out in his half-sleep:

When my Cue Comes, Call me and I will answer.

Half the comic effect comes from the alliteration of the three 'C's. If the 'C's are pointed, the audience laughs.

Assonance and Onomatopoeia

Assonance is the resemblance of sound between two syllables; it is the rhyming of one word with another in accented vowels but not in consonants. It alerts the actor to the richness of sound. Sometimes, indeed, Shakespeare plays with variations of it where the vowels chime like half-rhymes, as in Orsino's

O it came O'ER my EAR...

O'er and ear are almost a half-rhyme. The combination of vowel-correspondences with consonant-correspondences makes a vivid picture. Every page of Shakespeare demonstrates that he has a supremely well-tuned ear and that the music of the line is at one with its meaning. Onomatopoeia – a word that makes a sound similar to its meaning – infiltrates both alliteration and assonance. The sound is akin to what it describes:

Blow winds and CRACK your cheeks...
HOWL! HOWL! HOWL!

Paradox

Shakespeare's characters are constant wits. The sexual allure of Cleopatra is expressed by paradox:

she makes HUNGRY
Where most she SATISFIES...

Puns

Shakespeare loves to quibble on two similar words and so produce a pun, as in Lady Macbeth's

I'll GILD the faces of the grooms withal
For it must seem their GUILT.

The faces of the grooms are to be smeared with their life's blood, like gold on a statue. The presence of the blood will not only *gild* them, it will proclaim their part in the murder and demonstrate their *guilt*. 'Guilt' is therefore both golden and evil waiting to be punished.

Richard II quibbles at the moment of his greatest humiliation:

> In the BASE court: BASE court where Kings grow BASE
> To come at traitors' calls, and do them grace.

Hyperbole

Shakespeare is fond of showing tension by the use of hyperbole. It is an exaggeration which seeks to illuminate, or sometimes to denigrate, as in THE WINTER'S TALE where Paulina's grotesquely hyperbolical speech

> A thousand knees,
> Ten thousand years together, naked, fasting,
> Upon a barren mountain, and still winter
> In storm perpetual, could not move the gods
> To look that way thou wert...

parodies the extreme hyperbole with which Leontes expressed his groundless jealousy earlier in the play.

Personification

Allied to the use of hyperbole is personification:

> She sat like PATIENCE on a monument
> Smiling at grief...

To sum up
Rhetorical Devices

- *All these rhetorical devices are conscious inventions by the characters.*
- *The aim is to tell the audience their emotional state by illustrations and similarities.*

PRONUNCIATION

There is a central aspect of Shakespeare that time is inevitably altering: the actual *sound* of his speech. The pronunciation of English has naturally altered in the last four hundred years: language must always change and develop; it is part of the process of living. Our speech has become more clipped and constrained, less inflected and certainly peppered with more neutralised vowels. Every English vowel now aspires to the even greyness of 'er...' There is nothing the actor can do about this except appreciate that Shakespeare heard richer vowels and very percussive consonants (the 'K' was pronounced):

Doth not Brutus bootless Kneel

The Elizabethan vowels of 'Brewtus' and 'bewtless', as edgy as an oboe, are now also lost to us.

We have to consider how we can best express the musical potency of Shakespeare's text. A slightly increased joy in the sound of language, in the percussive nature of alliteration and the resonance of vowels must be attempted. But it must stop well short of affectation. And if it is based on the relish of the character rather than the actor, it will be more acceptable to our embarrassed-by-language age.

Direct communication remains one of the wonders of live theatre. And Shakespeare's theatre is public theatre – public stimulation. It provokes, cajoles and seduces the audience into imagining. For that reason, there is no soliloquy in Shakespeare where the actor muses privately to himself. Every soliloquy is indeed a public debate with the audience. Hamlet's 'To be or not to be' is a challenge to the audience; have they also ever contemplated suicide? Will they help him? Can they comment? All this keeps the soliloquy active and dramatic.

There is a further point to be made on pronunciation. For Shakespeare, variations in pronunciation were as common as variations in spelling. They were both illustrations of mood and responses to circumstance. There are therefore many varied pronunciations of the same word in Shakespeare. Coriolanus has three, if not four, different scansions:

What is it, CorioLANus must I call thee?

But this doesn't fit with:

> **Dost thou think**
> **I'll grace thee with that robbery, thy stolen name**
> **CorIolANus in CorIolI?**

There is also a constant need, if the scansion is to be preserved, to pronounce the 'i-on' in words like 'occasion' and 'confusion'. For Shakespeare they sometimes need two syllables:

> **Nor moody beggars starving for a time**
> **Of pell-mell havoc and confus-I-On.**
> (HENRY IV PART ONE, Act 5 Scene 1)

But this makes an affected and peculiar sound in modern English. It is, therefore, to be discouraged. It is possible by mutating the 'ion' into 'iern' to make it less affected, but the sound needs handling with great discretion. The rule in all these matters must be interpreted pragmatically. If it sounds silly, don't do it. Or more to the point, ask *why* it sounds silly and try to underplay it. The lack of a syllable in the scansion is sometimes more distorting than the archaic pronunciation. The rule is always follow what can be made to work, providing it fulfils the form.

BAWDY

Shakespeare's love of bawdy is evident throughout his work.

> **Mercutio**   …For the bawdy hand of the dial is
> now upon the prick of noon.

Yet his bawdiness is comprehensive and unself-conscious. It has indeed a joyous quality although it can contemplate what is disgusting when it needs to:

> **Hamlet**   Nay, but to live
> In the rank sweat of enseamèd bed,
> Stewed in corruption, honeying and making love
> Over the nasty sty…

It is certainly not true (as the nineteenth century wanted to believe) that Shakespeare was reluctant to be bawdy and only wrote filthily to please the popular audience. There is a zest in this filth which is irresistible and it is true to say that there is much more innuendo in his writing than any modern reader suspects or any modern audience comprehends. Many words in Shakespeare, from 'attempt' (to make a sexual approach) to 'yard' (a penis, usually with the implication of *penis erectus*), have a secondary sexual meaning that is now lost. The actor can only reflect that since sex is central to life, as a curse and a blessing and finally a great metaphor of creation, he must follow the comprehensiveness of his author.

THE ACTOR'S WORK ON HIMSELF

Having learned the clues and understood their usefulness, the actor must now consider himself. Acting Shakespeare is a highly physical business. The voice must be in good trim and as highly developed in range and resonance as the actor can manage. It is his primary instrument of communication when he acts Shakespeare. The richer the voice, the more individual its timbre, the greater the actor's expressiveness. The text – and by implication the voice that projects it – is the first means of communication in Shakespeare. There has never been a great Shakespearean actor with an unexciting voice. The word is the beginning and out of it comes the physical life of the character, the action and the atmosphere. Actors compensate for their voices in many ways. But for Shakespeare, every note that can be teased from the vocal cords will be needed.

I have stressed that the line structure must always be paramount. The actor should accordingly learn the ends of the lines when he learns the words. Breaths should only be taken at the end of the line. Breathing in the middle destroys the line. Modern actors are used to breathing when they naturally run out of breath. They then break up the text unthinkingly whenever their lungs need refilling. It is a personal and idiosyncratic need. But it does not do for Shakespeare. Because he requires the line structure to be preserved, he asks that the actor should always have enough breath in his lungs to deliver the full line. It is often possible for the actor to take a tiny breath at the end of the line to top up the supply of air. The lungs indeed should be for Shakespeare a kind of bagpipe – always full of air and always being replenished. The text can then be sustained and shaped.

On the other hand, the over-marking of the end of the lines is monotonous and quickly sends an audience to sleep. The line ending must be marked in a light, graceful and almost imperceptible fashion. And it should have an energy enshrined in an upward inflection which is always carrying us forward, filling us with expectation.

Shakespeare demands a defined breathing pattern which is not in any sense natural. It is not intended to be. In the early stages of rehearsal, it is important that the actor develops a pattern so that he knows on *which* end of line he needs to breathe. Breathing thus will aid the sense-phrasing which occurs at the end of each line. The pentameter is the unit of sense – and indeed the unit of communication. But if the audience don't sense where the end of the line is, they will not understand clearly. And if the actor does not know the end of the line, he will have no control over breath, voice, emotion or intent. To a greater or lesser degree, he will be incomprehensible. Allied to this controlled breathing is a mental state which makes it seem as if the character is inventing the words, relishing all the figures of speech and delighting in explaining himself by wit, paradox, pun and all the rest of the devices. This mental agility must be allied to a physical agility. Few men are capable of playing King Lear when they are as old as Lear should be. Few girls are capable of playing Juliet when they are young enough to appear fourteen. Lear has to *tell* about being old. Juliet has to *tell* about being young. Neither character is likely to be the right age. But then, although the play is not naturalistic, it must be credible enough to allow us to *imagine* the nature of age and the nature of youth.

If the actor is sharp in mind and alert in body, he can now proceed to the work on the text. The recognition of all the clues is work to be done by the actor by himself, or with the director during the very early stages of rehearsal. What has been set out so far is a map of the preparation, not the execution. To act Shakespeare without recognising these formal demands first is like trying to read a musical score when you have never heard a note of music.

So the key question must now be asked: once the actor has learned all the clues and where to find them, what does he do with them? He uses them actively and deliberately in order to communicate to his audience.

The character, as much as the actor, in Shakespeare is always aware that he is *telling* the story of himself and of the play by the images he invents, the rhythms he endorses, or the rhymes and accents, paradoxes and puns he invents. He is always conscious that he is *telling* – either to the other characters or to the audience. Therefore to relish what he invents gives energy and life to the text and emotional density to his character. It is public, often descriptive utterance. Finally, it is the personal creation of the actor as he makes, out of an infinite number of choices, what he says his own.

But there must remain a tension between the form and his freedom and that is why I continue to stress the parallel with jazz. Jazz musicians mean what they play. They must; they create it personally. Too many classical musicians simply play what somebody else means – what is written down. They are expert, but they are bland. They leave it to somebody else (usually the conductor) to provide the meaning. The same is unfortunately true of many classical actors who are competent but not original because they are simply repeating what somebody else has told them to do.

A jazz musician must mean something emotional in his own right – otherwise he has nothing to play. He is truly a soloist in embracing the form of the music (the rhythm, the harmonic progression, even the basic melody) and then improvising a personal response to all that he has been given. A great Shakespearean actor – Olivier at his best, Scofield at his best, Ashcroft at her best – is like a great jazz musician. The shape of the verse is meticulously preserved and the rhythm of the line is – just – respected. But, like Sidney Bechet, the articulation is always nearly *off* the beat. It is that instant of danger, of nearly being off, which makes the audience feel that the actor is natural and free. The process turns the formal into the natural and enables it to be natural and surprising. It no longer sounds like conventional Shakespeare when a master performs it because it is unexpected. The speech, the singing, the jazz become unique – made for this moment, unrepeatable. It can never be played quite like that again. The artificiality of the form – whether it be verbal, rhythmic, or musical – once more achieves a simulation of human reality. So great Shakespearean acting is not the dutiful repetition of a learned text with a specified rhythm. The act of defining the emotions in words and then telling them to an audience should seem for this moment only. There is a live engagement in this *telling*.

TELLING

There is always part of the actor which is monitoring what is being done during a performance. It registers whether he is communicating with the audience, advises him to wait for a laugh, and generally regulates the act of performing. This is a truism. It applies even more in Shakespeare because the consciousness of the actor is increased by the level of consciousness of the character. Hamlet *knows* that he is soliloquising to the audience and asking for their advice. Launce knows that he is finding fault with his dog in public. He demonstrates the dog's bad behaviour because he wants the audience to side with him. Romeo and Juliet know that as they fall in love with each other, they are telling their story to the audience. The Shakespearean *character* as well as the actor is self-aware, conscious of speaking blank verse, conscious of the form and aware of the effect he is making. All the rhetorical devices are built into the verse but they need reinventing by the individual actor. He invents them; he does not throw them away.

Telling a story, telling an action, telling the back history of the character, telling his future aspirations or fears – all these are the basis of Shakespeare's drama. Drama grew out of the Ancient Tribal Bards telling stories and the Sermonisers and Priests who narrated intricate prophesies. There can be no drama without a story: when the story falters, the audience's attention falters too. 'What happens next?' is the crucial question for any audience. If they have lost the desire to ask it, the play is dead. And they have literally lost the plot.

Shakespeare tells his story primarily by words. All his characters live in words and by the act of telling – and telling us – they invent images and metaphors that help us understand their loves and hates and confusions. Public soliloquy only turned into private soliloquy much later when the theatre invaded smaller spaces and was played by artificial light. Significantly, the convention of direct audience address – whether by speech or by aria – then began to wither. Baroque opera and Elizabethan drama is a public debate with a visible audience. No Shakespearean character should appear to know what he is going to say next. He must be spontaneous, and part of that spontaneity is the invention of a text which defines his emotional state. He invents images to describe his feelings, extraordinary phrases to explain himself. And that is the tension that keeps audiences hanging on his every word. The poet in Macbeth defines the psychology of a murderer being driven slowly mad by guilt, but he does it publicly and truthfully. There is no character who lies in soliloquy because he is talking honestly to the audience, his alter ego.

All Shakespeare's characters like talking. They enjoy defining themselves with a metaphor or a vivid adjective. They have an unquenchable relish for the sound and shape of words. The relish for words leads many of the characters to a love of wit. What is wit? It expresses contradictions or paradoxes in an apt, clever and unexpected way. It illuminates because it delights and stimulates an audience. It is often comic. The character must embody all this, as well as the actor. It is a complex distinction but an essential one for acting Shakespeare. So what kind of acting did Shakespeare like? What kind of performance was he aiming at? How did his actors *tell*?

Our only guide is Hamlet's Advice to the Players – a prose speech, but prose of great passion. It is of course dangerous to assume that a character in a play is expressing the opinions of his author. But Hamlet's enthusiasm for drama, spoken at such length, partly like a critic, partly like a director, seems to have the ring of Shakespeare himself. It shows Hamlet (suddenly not at all neurotic) for the first and only time at peace with himself. He reveals candidly what is important to him: acting. To act well is to define truth itself. He is absolutely unequivocal about his standards and his aims; and this is unusual for Hamlet. Surely this speech defines Shakespeare's own taste? And it is prose, not verse, because he is calm and rational.

> **Hamlet** Speak the speech I pray you as I pronounced it to
> you, trippingly on the tongue; but if you mouth
> it, as many of your players do, I had as lief the
> town crier had spoke my lines. Nor do not saw
> the air too much with your hand, thus, but use all
> gently; for in the very torrent, tempest, and as I
> may say the whirlwind of your passion, you must
> acquire and beget a temperance that may give it
> smoothness...   (HAMLET, Act 3 Scene 2)

Hamlet's definitions speak for themselves. Yet there is a painful paradox here. The popular cliché of the Shakespearean actor, with his loud bombast and singing inflections, is *exactly* what Hamlet – and we must believe, Shakespeare – objects to. And what on earth does 'smoothness' mean in this context? Balance? Restraint? Control? An avoidance of extreme dynamics or sudden jagged interruptions? Is it, therefore, however hot the speech may be, a reminder that it must remain controlled and contained enough so that the audience may understand it? The actor must not be 'over-the-top': he does not disturb with rage or repel with his tears. The extremes of emotion are delivered with control. The actor is not being indulgent and this 'smoothness' allows us to relate to him and understand him.

Hamlet continues:

> **Hamlet** ...O it offends me to the soul to hear a robustious periwig-pated fellow tear a passion to tatters, to very rags, to split the ears of the groundlings, who for the most part are capable of nothing but inexplicable dumb shows and noise. I would have such a fellow whipped for o'erdoing Termagant. It out-Herods Herod. Pray you avoid it.
>
> **First Player** I warrant your honour.
>
> **Hamlet** Be not too tame neither, but let your own discretion be your tutor. Suit the action to the word, the word to the action, with this special observance, that you o'erstep not the modesty of nature. For anything so overdone is from the purpose of playing whose end, both at the first and now, was and is to hold as 'twere the mirror up to nature, to show virtue her own feature, scorn her own image, and the very age and body of the time his form and pressure. Now this overdone, or come tardy off, though it make the unskilful laugh, cannot but make the judicious grieve; the censure of the which one must in your allowance o'erweigh a whole theatre of others. O there be players that I have seen play, and heard others praise, and that highly, not to speak it profanely, that neither having the accent of Christians nor the gait of Christian, Pagan, nor no man, have so strutted and bellowed that I have thought some of nature's journeymen had made men, and not made them well, they imitated humanity so abominably.

All directors know that to be dogmatic is to be dangerous. 'Be not too tame neither,' says Hamlet, immediately, with all the anxiety of a director who wants it both ways. 'I want you to be faster and yet slow enough to be comprehensible,' is the sort of contradictory final note that all directors indulge in. Hamlet continues: 'But let your own discretion be your tutor' – you must earn what can be emotional by your precision and your taste. *You*, you must decide how far you can go. Because what matters finally is that *you* do not 'o'erstep the modesty of nature' – what is fit, what is proper, what is unhysterical and finally, in acting terms, what is acceptable and above all sensible. There has to be discretion even in hysteria.

It has to be registered though that audiences tend to be excited by drama that is on the edge of the unacceptable. The danger point is very attractive. But every actor knows that audiences can be quickly lost if the performer topples over the edge.

So Hamlet gives us Shakespeare's style of acting confirmed: tripping speech, witty delivery, modest, temperate, perhaps cool – to use a word in modern parlance – as well as *smooth*. Yet it must be hot in its coolness, extreme in its discretion. Finally, of course, 'smoothness' must refer to the line of the iambic text. It is smooth because it is controlled, controlled because it is temperate. Its structure must be observed and its flow maintained. There must be no sudden szforzandos or misaccents in the line. Only by being smooth is it capable *occasionally* of communicating the rough.

Here is the paradox: by hiding the feeling you reveal it; by *not* indulging it, you express it. This is the contradiction in all great acting. Perhaps it is the ambiguity in all great art. The feeling may be a very torrent, a tempest, a whirlwind; but the audience needs an utterance which is controlled and considered in order to receive it.

But be not too tame neither…

THE EXTRACTS

Apart from the first extract, which is to get us into the swing of things, the following speeches are arranged in chronological order.

The Analytical Notes are an attempt to set out what the actor should look for when he first meets the speech. They therefore analyse the words he is to speak and, to a large extent, the way he is to speak them.

All the extracts have been freshly edited by Roger Warren for this book from the original texts. The punctuation is lighter than would be required by strictly grammatical modern usage, in order to preserve the structure and rhythm of the lines as much as possible and not distract the actor. The scene numbers are those of the Oxford Shakespeare (1986), and the conjectural dates of composition those of its Textual Companion (1987), both volumes edited by Stanley Wells and Gary Taylor.

SPEECHES FOR ANALYSIS

Love's Labour's Lost
(1594–5)
Act 5 Scene 2
Mercadé and the
Princess of France

Then in chronological order:
The Two Gentlemen
of Verona
(1590–1)
Act 2 Scene 3
Launce and his dog

Love's Labour's Lost
(1594–5)
Act 3 Scene 1
Berowne

Romeo and Juliet
(1595)
Act 1 Scene 3
The Nurse

Romeo and Juliet
(1595)
Act 5 Scene 3
The Prince and Friar
Laurence

A Midsummer
Night's Dream
(1595)
Act 2 Scene 1
Oberon and Puck

Henry IV Part One
(1596–7)
Act 2 Scene 5
Falstaff and Prince Hal

Julius Caesar
(1599)
Act 3 Scene 2
Brutus and the Plebeians

Twelfth Night
(1601)
Act 1 Scene 1
Orsino and Curio

Twelfth Night
(1601)
Act 1 Scene 5
Viola and Olivia

Hamlet
(1601)
Act 3 Scene 3
Claudius and Hamlet

Hamlet
(1601)
Act 3 Scene 4
Hamlet and Gertrude

Measure for Measure
(1603)
Act 2 Scene 2
Angelo

Othello
(1603–4)
Act 5 Scene 2
Othello

Macbeth
(1606)
Act 2 Scene 1
Macbeth

Antony and Cleopatra
(1606)
Act 5 Scene 2
Cleopatra

The Winter's Tale
(1609)
Act 1 Scene 2
Leontes

The Winter's Tale
(1609)
Act 3 Scene 2
Hermione and Leontes

The Winter's Tale
(1609)
Act 4 Scene 1
Time

The Tempest
(1611)
Act 5 Scene 1
Prospero

The Tempest
(1611)
Epilogue
Prospero

Shakespeare's Epitaph

LOVE'S LABOUR'S LOST
ACT 5 SCENE 2

Mercadé God save you, madam.

Princess   Welcome, Mercadé,
But that thou interrupt'st our merriment.

Mercadé I am sorry madam, for the news I bring
Is heavy in my tongue. The King your father –

Princess Dead, for my life.

Mercadé   Even so. My tale is told.

Berowne Worthies away. The scene begins to cloud.

LOVE'S LABOUR'S LOST
ACT 5 SCENE 2

This is one of the most heart-tugging moments in all Shakespeare. It is simple and concise, but has to be phrased as it is written and not distorted by other rhythms. It is a perfect example of how the form can lead the actor to acknowledge what he will have to feel; and it is therefore excellent for the first analysis.

The proximity of death in life suddenly confronts a group of young people who have hitherto thought that time had no hold on them. The young Shakespeare achieves an astonishing change of mood by the manipulation of his verse. He is already a master.

I have stressed that the actor can never break the line, or pause during it, unless there is a caesura. If the punctuation suggests a slight pause at the caesura, it must be earned by taking a moderate-to-slow tempo on the first half of the line, matching it after the caesura and thus making the two halves one. This gives time for the caesura break. Nonetheless, the shape of the line must be preserved and that should be the actor's main concern. To pause at the *end* of the line is always permissible if the sense allows it, and providing that the pause has been earned by the strength of the dramatic situation.

LOVE'S LABOUR'S LOST is nearing its close. Four young noblemen, including the King, have vowed to dedicate themselves to study. They have therefore forsworn the company of women and the pursuit of love. During the play, their resolve has weakened and they have endured many comic trials. Here, having broken their vows, they are just about to engage themselves to four beautiful ladies, including the young Princess, when a messenger arrives from her Court.

Mercadé enters with a conventional greeting, and the Princess answers him equally graciously and completes the half-line on cue. There might even be a shade of reproof in her second line; or perhaps she is just slightly bewildered, instinctively feeling that this solemn figure should not be here. Is all well?

Mercadé, as befits a messenger with tragic news, speaks simply and unemotionally. He uses straightforward colloquial speech. The actor should notice that the end of the line with the word 'bring' sets up a major change of pace on the next caesura line. 'Is heavy in my tongue' is very slow so that the full stop can be accommodated and the news of the King can be given in a measured way.

I believe that Mercadé stops at the end of his speech unable to go on. After the word 'father', there is an enormous pause while the Princess realises what he is trying to say.

Mercadé God save you, madam.

Princess   Welcome, Mercadé,
But that thou interrupt'st our merriment.

Mercadé I am sorry madam, for the news I bring
Is heavy in my tongue. **The King your father –**

Princess Dead, for my life.

Mercadé   **Even so. My tale is told.**

Berowne Worthies away. The scene begins to cloud.

I believe this is an accurate interpretation because if the Princess comes in quickly and nervously on the cue, it is impossible for Mercadé to complete the subsequent half line. Apart from anything else, he simply hasn't time to adjust his thoughts.

The long pause after 'father' allows us to watch the Princess in close-up, as she gradually senses what Mercadé is about to say. 'Dead, for my life' is her intuition, slow and monosyllabic. Mercadé comes in on cue and completes the line with the same tempo and gravity. The actor should lean slightly on the plaintive alliteration of '**T**ale' and '**T**old'.

Another way of performing this exchange (and one which I have frequently seen in the theatre) works less well and destroys Shakespeare's verse structure. If the Princess takes the cue quickly, nervously putting words into Mercadé's mouth, then he has to hold a long pause before 'Even so. My tale is told.' But this is a predictable rhythm which cannot help verging on the sentimental. More to the point, it completely ruins the linear discipline of the verse, and to little purpose. If Shakespeare had wanted such a shape, he would have written it by using half lines that have no completion. He has carefully done the opposite.

Berowne concludes this chilling exchange by comparing it to the sun being unexpectedly covered with clouds. The whole passage is a miracle of form – a form that expresses a full dramatic situation. This is Shakespeare's advice to the players in action.

THE TWO GENTLEMEN OF VERONA
ACT 2 SCENE 3

(enter Launce with his dog, Crab)

Launce Nay, 'twill be this hour ere I have done weeping.
All the kind of the Launces have this very fault.
I have received my proportion, like the prodigious
son, and am going with Sir Proteus to the Imperial's
court. I think Crab, my dog, be the sourest-natured
dog that lives. My mother weeping, my father wailing,
my sister crying, our maid howling, our cat wringing
her hands, and all our house in a great perplexity, yet
did not this cruel-hearted cur shed one tear. He is a
stone, a very pebble-stone, and has no more pity in
him than a dog. A Jew would have wept to have seen
our parting. Why, my grandam, having no eyes, look
you, wept herself blind at my parting. Nay, I'll show
you the manner of it. This shoe is my father. No, this
left shoe is my father. No, no, this left shoe is my
mother. Nay, that cannot be so, neither. Yes, it is so,
it is so, it hath the worser sole. This shoe with the hole
in it is my mother, and this my father. A vengeance
on't, there 'tis. Now sir, this staff is my sister, for, look
you, she is as white as a lily and as small as a wand.
This hat is Nan our maid. I am the dog. No, the dog
is himself, and I am the dog. O, the dog is me, and I
am myself. Ay, so, so…

THE TWO GENTLEMEN OF VERONA
ACT 2 SCENE 3

In this scene, Launce, the Servant and the Clown, introduces his dog Crab to the audience. He speaks in prose, but it is prose designed to manipulate an audience and provide laughter. This is a comic monologue in an English tradition that runs from the Mystery Plays through Shakespeare and the Restoration, to the Music Hall and the stand-up comics of our own time. It is verbal humour at its most assured.

THE TWO GENTLEMEN OF VERONA is an early play; indeed, some critics think it is Shakespeare's first. Nonetheless, the dramatist is already wise in the techniques of popular comedy and the verbal rhythms that prompt the laughter of an audience. Comedy is always about timing: the performer either surprises the audience, or fulfils their hopes with the expected. But he can only succeed if the rhythm of the line provokes the laugh.

Launce leads on his dog. He is weeping; he has just said farewell to his family. Everybody was in tears except the dog – so the dog is clearly heartless.

The notion of conducting a scene with a dog is of course comic genius. It would be impossible for two people to play a duologue with a dog present because he would inevitably distract. But with the dog and one actor, the dog becomes the straight man in a cross-talk act. He is the stooge. If he does nothing, the actor can time the laugh off the dog's lack of reaction. And if he makes any movement – rolling his eyes, scratching his ears, wagging his tail – there is likely to be an even bigger laugh. Any action is a comment. And so is the lack of any action.

The whole speech is an assessment of the dog's qualities before a public forum – the audience. He did not weep at the farewells and he is not weeping now. Launce is asking for the audience's judgement on the dog as well as their sympathy and understanding for himself.

Shakespeare's comic prose always has a strong rhythmic base which the actor must ride. This is partly produced by antithesis, partly by alliteration. Much of Shakespeare's topical comedy writing has necessarily lost its edge as its meaning becomes more obscure. But the rhythm of the writing is so strong that it can still produce laughter from audiences when they are not absolutely sure what the line means. Because the rhythm announces a laugh, it arrives. The alliteration of 'Proportion', 'Prodigious', 'Proteus', 'ImPerial', gives a self-righteousness to the line which helps Launce recover from his crying. 'Prodigious' is of course a verbal mistake for 'Prodigal'. A modern actor

Nay, 'twill be this hour ere I have done weeping.
All the kind of the Launces have this very fault.
I have received my proportion, like the prodigious
son, and I am going with Sir Proteus to the Imperial's
court. I think Crab, my dog, be the sourest-natured
dog that lives. My mother weeping, my father wailing,
my sister crying, our maid howling, our cat wringing
her hands, and all our house in a great perplexity, yet
did not **this cruel-hearted cur** shed one tear.

must not be shy of these mistakes. 'Prodigious' here is a boast that links with 'Proportion'. He was a son who was particularly well-endowed.

Launce has entered crying and continues to cry until he gets some reaction from his audience. Then, with the air of a man who is informing us that we have not heard anything yet, he points out that he will be making this noise for the next hour. It is a family failing. They are very emotional people, the Launces. Then he pulls rank with the pomposity of the alliterative line: Sir Proteus has been selected for the Imperial Court. He now returns to the dog.

The dog needs careful casting. If Crab is a sweet and amiable dog, there is an immediate comic tension between the audience's sympathy for him and Launce's criticisms of his cur-like behaviour. But the scene can work equally well with a miserable-looking dog. Launce tells us that this is the sourest natured of dogs. He then embarks on a long sentence full of antithetical phrases, where his mother weeps, his father wails, his sister cries, the maid howls and then (to our surprise) the cat wrings her hands – a mistake which brings comic bathos. The actor must not wait for a laugh, but press on to the climax where the 'Cruel-hearted Cur' (alliteration again, delivering the emphasis) refuses to shed one tear. It is the pay-off of the climax of grief after an enormous build. An amiable-looking dog adds to the comedy as the long list of weepers is balanced antithetically by this dry-eyed, cheerful cur. Providing the actor pushes on to the end of the sentence, the rhythm of the writing will announce and then deliver the laugh.

This defines another rule of the prose speeches. Whether the speech is high-born, rational and fanciful, or the words of the uneducated pretending to know more than they do, it is vital to play the entire sentence through to the full stop. By this means, the rhythms of each phrase can answer each other. To divide up the prose sentences in order to get laughs is self-defeating. It will assuredly spoil the big laugh that Shakespeare has carefully provided at the end of the sentence.

To Launce, the dog is not a dog but a person. He finds it easy to criticise the dog for having no more pity than a dog – a term of abuse. This is the normal pejorative use of the word. 'Dog' is usually an insult, a person seen as a dog is a cur who is by instinct unfaithful and treacherous. Indeed in later Shakespeare, the dog is a fawning, treacherous hypocritical animal who lives under the table in the great hall in the hope of unexpected food. By the time he wrote HAMLET, Shakespeare did not like dogs, and there is contempt in 'Let the candied tongue lick absurd pomp...'

He is a stone, a very pebble-stone, and has no more pity in him than a dog. **A Jew would have wept to have seen our parting.** Why, my grandam, having no eyes, look you, wept herself blind at my parting. Nay, I'll show you the manner of it. This shoe is my father. No, this left shoe is my father. No, no, this left shoe is my mother. Nay, that cannot be so, neither. Yes, it is so, it is so, it hath the worser sole. This shoe with the hole in it is my mother, and this my father. **A vengeance on't, there 'tis.** Now sir, this staff is my sister, for, look you, she is as white as a lily and as small as a wand. This hat is Nan our maid. I am the dog. **No, the dog is himself, and I am the dog.** O, the dog is me, and I am myself. Ay, so, so…

Launce moves on from 'cur' to 'Jew' as a further term of abuse. It is not at all politically correct. He then caps it all with a sick joke. He tells us that though his grandmother is blind, she manages metaphorically to weep herself blind at his parting. It is a grotesque image. This comedy is never sentimental.

From here on, the prose takes on a more practical, colloquial rhythm. Launce decides to demonstrate the drama of his farewell from his family by using his shoes. The pun on 'sole', which also means 'soul', is conscious on Launce's part and develops into the ancient Christian jibe against womanhood. Our Mother Eve is criticised again.

The routine with the shoes is again balanced in its rhythms. Its precision is worthy of Samuel Beckett. Launce begins with the right shoe as his father, thus recognising the supremacy of the male. But because it has a hole in it, he reluctantly has to give precedence to the left. Yet his father cannot be second in line and be the left shoe. The left shoe *must* be his mother. He is then grieved that the damaged shoe is his mother. But he takes comfort that this is allowable because she has the worser soul/sole. And then to cap it all he cheers himself up with a dirty joke, concluding that the mother, as the female, must have the hole in it. Eve is the more sinful: because her genitals are represented by the hole in the shoe.

He then loses patience with the whole demonstration ('A vengeance on't, there 'tis') and moves into a more tender and sentimental tone. He invokes his sister, and uses his white staff to demonstrate her lily-like graciousness. He takes his hat off and something about it – either its bulk or perhaps its pertness – makes him think that it represents Nan, the maid. He has taken the hat off. Now he can be the dog. But then he realises that this is an unnecessary impersonation because the real dog is already there, looking at him. He has a dog already. The dog is the dog.

The next line ('No, the dog is himself and I am the dog') puns on the word 'dog'. The dog is himself, but Launce by his grief and dismay has himself been reduced to a mere cur, a victim. He goes on with this thought that indeed the dog is him and that he has been reduced by suffering. The 'so, so' confirms his cur-like status.

During all this free improvisation, using the available props, Launce has frequently forgotten the dog, who has been sitting there unheeded. But if his reactions interrupt Launce's speech, Launce can deal with him, play the audience reaction, and then go back with renewed vigour to his story. Anything can happen with a dog. And it does. A protracted fit of scratching can bring the house down. The dog gives the scene an

THE TWO GENTLEMEN OF VERONA, Royal Shakespeare Company 1960.
Patrick Wymark as Launce, with Crab. In background, Jack MacGowran (Speed).

immediacy and a danger which is a comic contrast to the high-flown emotions of the young lovers in this play.

The pay-off again is the dog. Launce, having reduced himself to a miserable dog, realises that the one thing he has in life is a dog. Launce doesn't relish the insult of calling himself a dog. But absurdly enough a dog is the only thing he has that's real. So the 'Ay, so, so' is relief that he has found all his props, defined his imaginings and prepared for his story. He now tells it with maximum drama and maximum complication. Whatever the dog does through all this grief and wailing is mundane and will undercut the melodrama comically.

If the verse is to be spoken **trippingly**, the prose must be spoken **pointedly**. The primary need in speaking prose is to feel the rhythm of the sentence so that the requisite words can be emphasised in order to point the paradoxes and the comparisons. Each joke will then naturally have its 'feed' and then its pay-off where the laugh will occur. The main action of the scene is to try to make the audience disapprove of the dog and side with Launce. It never does. However hard Launce weeps there is no sympathy. He then tells us that the whole family wept except the dog. Still he receives no sympathy. He is then driven to a desperate demonstration of how the scene became more and more emotional using any props that are to hand.

The whole scene builds to a climax of insensitivity. Finally Launce achieves nothing because his sorry story is interrupted by the entrance of Proteus before he can finish it. It is an awful anticlimax.

LOVE'S LABOUR'S LOST

ACT 3 SCENE 1

Berowne And I, forsooth, in love – I that have been love's whip,
A very beadle to a humorous sigh,
A critic, nay, a night-watch constable,
A domineering pedant o'er the boy,
Than whom no mortal so magnificent.
This wimpled, whining, purblind, wayward boy,
This Signor Junior, giant dwarf, Dan Cupid,
Regent of love-rhymes, lord of folded arms,
Th'anointed sovereign of sighs and groans,
Liege of all loiterers and malcontents,
Dread prince of plackets, king of codpieces,
Sole imperator and great general
Of trotting paritors – O my little heart!
And I to be a corporal of his field,
And wear his colours like a tumbler's hoop!
What? I love, I sue, I seek a wife? –
A woman that is like a German clock,
Still a-repairing, ever out of frame,
And never going aright, being a watch,
But being watched that it may still go right.
Nay to be perjured, which is worst of all,
And among three to love the worst of all –
A whitely wanton with a velvet brow
With two pitch-balls stuck in her face for eyes;
Ay, and by heaven, one that will do the deed
Though Argus were her eunuch and her guard.
And I to sigh for her, to watch for her,
To pray for her – go to, it is a plague
That Cupid will impose for my neglect
Of his almighty dreadful little might.
Well, I will love, write, sigh, pray, sue, and groan;
Some men must love my lady, and some Joan.

LOVE'S LABOUR'S LOST
ACT 3 SCENE 1

Berowne is in the classic position of all young men in love. He knows he is absurd. He swears that he is not interested in women; that he will never be in love, never lovesick, never be dependent on a woman. And he has repeated this time and time again, though he knows in his heart of hearts that there is a part of him he cannot control. Now it has happened. He is in love, and is not only amazed at himself, but dismayed at himself as well. He is very ready to share his weakness with the audience, but it is humiliating all the same. His dismay is expressed in a defiant soliloquy in early Shakespearean 'end-stopped' verse. Here are no caesuras to be used in the subtle, pace-changing way of the later verse; no hesitations, and few irregularities. Yet there is a colloquial vigour in his indignation which is in sharp contrast to the regular verse form which rides on it. It is comic, contradictory and very muscular. The actor must have a quick tongue and it must answer to a quick brain.

Line 1 has too many syllables, and thus too many feet. The words come out in a great splurge:

And I, forsooth, in love – I that have been love's whip...

The line has six feet instead of five, and is largely monosyllabic. 'That have' is elided so that it makes only one syllable – and the monosyllabic nature of the line may lead the actor to a sense of amazement with himself.

In line 2, a 'beadle' is a parish officer or local policeman. Berowne is comparing himself to the Watch, and then to the Schoolmaster and then to a Critic – not a critic in our sense of the word, but a general fault-finder – a misanthrope. He had sought to eradicate love (as represented by the boy Cupid) from his life. This boy is everywhere and is everything paradoxical – big, yet little; strong, yet weak. Berowne builds his indignation through insult after insult, sustained by explosive alliteration: ('**P**rince of **P**lackets', '**K**ing of **C**od-pieces'). The speech is all one vast exclamation mark, and although the verse is reasonably regular and has colloquial energy and an everyday use of vocabulary, it still feels dangerous and hectic, as if the train is liable to come off the rails because its progress is too fast, too headlong. The verse never does derail, of course, but the tension is constant.

'Sole I**m**perator' is inflected abnormally so that the line scans. A mocking attitude to the word and to the 'great general' make this oddity of scansion expressive.

The mood of the speech breaks on the monosyllabic line ('What? I love, I sue, I seek a wife?') which, as it were, puts Berowne's love on the table unblinkingly, ready for

A woman that is like a German clock,
Still a-repairing, ever out of frame,
And never going aright, being a watch,
But being watched that it may still go right.
Nay to be perjured, which is worst of all,
And among three to love the worst of all –
A whitely wanton with a velvet brow
With two pitch-balls stuck in her face for eyes;
Ay, and by heaven, one that will do the deed
Though Argus were her eunuch and her guard.
And I to sigh for her, to watch for her,
To pray for her – go to, it is a plague
That Cupid will impose for my neglect
Of his almighty dreadful little might.
Well, I will love, write, sigh, pray, sue, and groan;
Some men must love my lady, and some Joan.

scrutiny. He now tries ridicule in order to cauterise himself. A woman is like a German clock and is always going wrong – in both senses of the word, morally and mechanically. And there is a further shrewd pun on the word 'watch'. Like a watch, a man watches a woman to see that she is going properly (walking decorously and to a proper destination). And because she is constantly watched, she has to go 'right'. Meanwhile, the alliteration continues to sustain the wit – 'Whitely Wanton', 'Do the Deed'. He describes her physical appearance as grossly as possible ('two pitch balls stuck in her face for eyes') in order to denigrate her. She must not seem attractive to him. And this leads him to a monosyllabic ('heaven' is elided) admission that his lady has strong, sensual appetites. The line condemns and excites, repels and attracts:

> **Ay, and by heaven, one that will do the deed**
> **Though Argus were her eunuch and her guard.**

The sexual thought gives us the pointed word 'deed' at the end of the line; and the hyperbole of Argus (the giant with a hundred eyes) as a eunuch caps it all.

As the speech winds to its end, it uses more and more monosyllabic lines: Berowne's depth of true feeling is showing and the lines are accordingly spread. The paradox of Cupid as someone dreadful (that is, capable of filling us with dread – the quibble is ghoulish), someone little, yet someone mighty, continues.

The final couplet admits defeat. Whether we love a fine lady or a plain Joan, we still love and the madness is unquestionable. It is a fever that Berowne and his fellows must come to terms with. The self-discovery is full of mockery: it rejects what it celebrates, and celebrates what it rejects. It is the very heart of the play, as it is of so much of early Shakespeare: **'The lunatic, the lover and the poet / Are of imagination all compact...'** (A MIDSUMMER NIGHT'S DREAM, Act 5 Scene 1).

Here we have colloquial verse which expresses the character's wit, his self-knowledge, his love of women and words and his comic dismay with himself. It is a true confessional. In a few years time, the same observation will produce Benedick.

ROMEO AND JULIET

ACT 1 SCENE 3

Nurse Even or odd, of all days in the year
Come Lammas Eve at night shall she be fourteen.
Susan and she – God rest all Christian souls! –
Were of an age. Well, Susan is with God;
She was too good for me. But as I said,
On Lammas Eve at night shall she be fourteen,
That shall she, marry, I remember it well.
'Tis since the earthquake now eleven years,
And she was weaned – I never shall forget it –
Of all the days of the year upon that day,
For I had then laid wormwood to my dug,
Sitting in the sun under the dovehouse wall.
My lord and you were then at Mantua.
Nay, I do bear a brain! But as I said,
When it did taste the wormwood on the nipple
Of my dug and felt it bitter, pretty fool,
To see it tetchy and fall out wi' th' dug!
'Shake', quoth the dove-house! 'Twas no need, I trow
To bid me trudge;
And since that time it is eleven years,
For then she could stand high-lone. Nay, by th' rood,
She could have run and waddled all about,
For even the day before, she broke her brow,
And then my husband – God be with his soul,
A was a merry man! – took up the child.
'Yea' quoth he, 'dost thou fall upon thy face?
Thou wilt fall backward when thou hast more wit,
Wilt thou not, Jule?' And by my halidom,
The pretty wretch left crying and said 'Ay'.

ROMEO AND JULIET
ACT 1 SCENE 3

This is the first time we meet Juliet's Nurse in the play. Perhaps to our surprise, she speaks in blank verse – largely because those around her (Lady Capulet, Juliet and Capulet himself) also speak in verse. The Nurse speaks in prose for much of the rest of the play, but here she speaks 'proper' as her betters do, by using verse. Yet it is verse that can use the idiomatic vocabulary of a peasant, when it is called for.

Shakespeare knows that there is nothing to be gained here by switching from prose to verse and from verse back to prose. The other characters are waiting for the Nurse to get to the point. And she takes her iambic time.

The other originality of the speech is that Shakespeare is inventing a particular language – colloquial, repetitive and garrulous. It creates a character in recognisable flesh-and-blood terms. He is always capable of creating a 'voice' for a character. Even early on – in Richard III's ironic hyperboles, or Henry VI's wry, sad truisms – we are dealing with a dramatist who can completely express characters by the particularity of their speech. Holofernes, the schoolmaster, and Don Armado, the Don Quixote of LOVE'S LABOUR'S LOST, have particular and ornate speech patterns which bring them to life. In quite different ways, Othello, Falstaff, Macbeth, Leontes all have verbal individuality. But the actor should recognise that Shakespeare is quite eclectic in this use of speech. Sometimes he hears a particular voice and writes it, as when he sets the wry colloquialisms of the Bastard Falconbridge against the rhetorical formality of the politicians in KING JOHN. At other times, he settles for the neutrality of a plain narrative style (usually expressed in straightforward verse) until the eccentric and individual voice of a great character steps on to the stage.

The Nurse's speech is an example of this individuality. It is a piece of virtuoso writing. Here is a peasant woman who loves the sound of her own voice. She is garrulous and invokes memories because they make her feel important. Above all, she adores the family and the child – Juliet – that she has been Nurse to and looked after for years. She is a creature of proverbs, country saws, of naïve Christian faith. In this faith, we can hear the common people of Warwickshire chattering over a water-pump or gossiping in a shop. Yet Shakespeare transforms this demotic speech into a blank verse which keeps the energy going and the expectation high. The verse sustains the comedy and encourages the repetitions. And the actor will need to push on with the speech, so that the loquaciousness maintains its power. This Nurse is not to be easily interrupted.

The speech begins with monosyllables which correct Lady Capulet. How ever long is it to Lammastide? At Lammas Eve, Juliet will be fourteen. As the speech develops,

Even or odd, of all days in the year
Come Lammas Eve at night shall she be fourteen.
Susan and she – God rest all Christian souls! –
Were of an age. Well, Susan is with God;
She was too good for me. But as I said,
On Lammas Eve at night shall she be fourteen,
That shall she, marry, I remember it well.
'Tis since the earthquake now eleven years,
And she was weaned – I never shall forget it –
Of all the days of the year upon that day,
For I had then laid wormwood to my dug,
Sitting in the sun under the dovehouse wall.
My lord and you were then at Mantua.
Nay, I do bear a brain! But as I said,
When it did taste the wormwood on the nipple
Of my dug and felt it bitter, pretty fool,
To see it tetchy and fall out wi' th' dug!
'Shake', quoth the dove-house! 'Twas no need, I trow
To bid me trudge;
And since that time it is eleven years,
For then she could stand high-lone. Nay, by th' rood,
She could have run and waddled all about,
For even the day before, she broke her brow,
And then my husband – God be with his soul,
A was a merry man! – took up the child.
'Yea' quoth he, 'dost thou fall upon thy face?
Thou wilt fall backward when thou hast more wit,
Wilt thou not, Jule?' And by my halidom,
The pretty wretch left crying and said 'Ay'.

Shakespeare changes pace and tacks on several caesura breaks as new memories come flooding in. With each of them comes a change of tone and tempo. The sense that the Nurse will never get to the end of the story grows and grows as dependent clause follows dependent clause and line caps line. She loves her memories and she is big-hearted. Suddenly there is a lyrical line which conjures up a whole picture and, by the use of the trochee at its start, compels our attention:

Sitting in the sun under the dovehouse wall

There is a half-line pause on

To bid me trudge

– which (I believe) is an invitation to the actor to delight for a moment in the memory. The wonder then carries on into the next line –

And since that time it is eleven years

which is full of the awe with which we all contemplate the inexplicable passing of time. The years fly by at a pace that we find hard to accept.

The Nurse then achieves the point of her rambling story: the slightly naughty joke about the girl growing into the sexually active woman and falling backwards. She is so delighted with this that she repeats it. People do when they like their own jokes.

What is extraordinary about this passage is that it sounds like naturalistic speech. Yet it isn't. Its iambic rhythms observe all the rules which more formal speeches show in analysis. And the actor will find that by observing the rhythm, something is created that sounds naturalistic. Yet its ongoing energy makes it a delight to act and to listen to. It is immediately recognisable in human terms.

Is it poetry? Well yes, because of its warmth and its humanity. Is it dramatic verse? Certainly. It captivates an audience. The demands of the verse and the demands of the garrulous self-important character are fused into one. To ignore the verse structure and turn it into prose will make it sound artificial. By carefully observing the form, it will sound 'real' and natural.

ROMEO AND JULIET

ACT 5 SCENE 3

Prince   Bring forth the parties of suspicion.

Friar Laurence   I am the greatest, able to do least,
Yet most suspected, as the time and place
Doth make against me, of this direful murder;
And here I stand, both to impeach and purge
Myself condemnèd and myself excused.

Prince   Then say at once what thou dost know in this.

Friar Laurence   I will be brief, for my short date of breath
Is not so long as is a tedious tale.
Romeo, there dead, was husband to that Juliet,
And she, there dead, that Romeo's faithful wife.
I married them, and their stol'n marriage day
Was Tybalt's doomsday, whose untimely death
Banished the new-made bridegroom from this city,
For whom, and not for Tybalt, Juliet pined.
You, to remove that siege of grief from her,
Betrothed and would have married her perforce
To County Paris. Then comes she to me,
And with wild looks bid me devise some mean
To rid her from this second marriage,
Or in my cell there would she kill herself.
Then gave I her – so tutored by my art –
A sleeping potion, which so took effect
As I intended, for it wrought on her
The form of death. Meantime I writ to Romeo
That he should hither come as this dire night
To help to take her from her borrowed grave,
Being the time the potion's force should cease.
But he which bore my letter, Friar John,
Was stayed by accident, and yesternight
Returned my letter back.

ROMEO AND JULIET
ACT 5 SCENE 3

This is a mesmerising example of early Shakespearean verse – speedy, economical in its imagery and telling a complicated story with economical rapidity. The first question the actor will ask is: 'Why is the story told at all?' Or rather 'Why is the story told again?' The speech occurs at the end of the play when all the action is over. The audience have seen everything that it details, and there is not one surprise in it. It is also therefore no surprise that this speech (or most of it) is usually cut in the theatre.

But the cut does great damage to Friar Laurence's character and to the moral integrity of the play. Friar Laurence has been tempted to meddle with destiny in order to save Juliet from a bigamous marriage and a threatened suicide. He therefore decides to use his 'art' (his work with herbs and medicines) to make her seem dead. Then at his command, and at a suitable moment, he will resurrect her. For good reasons, he is tempted to commit this ultimate blasphemy as if he were presiding at the Day of Judgement. And he succumbs to the temptation. The Herbalist plays God, as Prospero does in THE TEMPEST later.

By the end of the play, the Friar realises that in meddling in matters of life and death and presuming to control them, he has committed the greatest sin that a holy man could contemplate. This desperate speech is his attempt to shrive himself. He confesses so that he may be cleansed of sin.

The Friar states his purpose in the first lines:

> … both to impeach and purge
> Myself condemnèd and myself excused.

This speech is his repentance; and to a religious audience, his need for atonement would have been acutely understandable. He confesses the sins he has been tempted to commit. The Friar's hubris in playing God has brought disaster and tragedy to the very people that he sought to save. Man cannot play God and go unpunished.

But Shakespeare knows that to repeat this story at the end of the play is a dangerous risk to take with any audience. The rapidity and clarity of this verse obviously comes from this knowledge. He has a great need to sustain interest and save time. There is also another need: in character terms the speech only works if it is born of emotional desperation – of the Friar's urgent desire to confess and be forgiven.

The repeated '**there, dead**' sounds the consequences of the Friar's actions: they seem ineradicable as sins. The '**husband**' chimes with the 'faithful **wife**'; and 'the **marriage day**' with 'Tybalt's **doomsday**'.

You, to remove that siege of grief from her,
Betrothed and would have married her perforce
To County Paris. Then comes she to me,
And with wild looks bid me devise some mean
To rid her from this second marriage,
Or in my cell there would she kill herself.
Then gave I her – so tutored by my art –
A sleeping potion, which so took effect
As I intended, for it wrought on her
The form of death. Meantime I writ to Romeo
That he should hither come as this dire night
To help to take her from her borrowed grave,
Being the time the potion's force should cease.
But he which bore my letter, Friar John,
Was stayed by accident, and yesternight
Returned my letter back.

The verse rushes on to the caesura where there is a change of pace on 'To County Paris'. The Friar is very conscious of the enormity of what he is saying. It is because of County Paris that Juliet comes to visit the Friar. One horror prepares for another.

The scansion of this line is interesting:

To COUNty PARis. THEN comes SHE to ME

The clumsiness expresses the Friar's emotional state. He is fighting to keep control. And the scansion gives a strong accent on 'me' which points clearly to the Friar's full guilt and responsibility.

The 'art' to which the Friar confesses is near to the black magic of the alchemist, and it produces in Juliet something unnatural: 'The form of death'. The admission comes at the second caesura when a change of pace is enforced on the speech. A complete line in one tempo has to be made of:

The form of death. Meantime I writ to Romeo…

It is very slow if it is to accommodate the horror of the admissions and the break at the full stop. Perhaps the Friar is awed. The whole line is haunted. The next line regains the hectic pace.

There is a return to the narrative pace in the next line. And the third caesura change of pace comes at the end of this extract:

Returned my letter back.

It is difficult to imagine how these terrible events could be confessed more clearly; nor how they could be expressed more economically. The speaker is in torment as he tells them. The grave is 'borrowed', the letter is delayed by 'accident'. Everything is unnatural – the product of blasphemy. It is the purging of a holy man, a lover of healing who has not healed but destroyed. If Shakespeare had used his heavily balanced prose, he would not easily have been able to create this headlong rush of anguish, spoken directly from the heart.

ROMEO AND JULIET, Center Theatre Group at the Ahmanson Theatre, Los Angeles 2001.
Michael Gross as Friar Laurence and D B Woodside as Romeo.

The Friar finishes:

> **if aught in this**
> **Miscarried by my fault, let my old life**
> **Be sacrificed some hour before his time,**
> **Unto the rigour of severest law.**

His confession is complete. But is he shriven? We never know what happens to this blasphemous man who was tempted to manipulate life and death – albeit for very human reasons. The Prince says:

> **Some shall be pardoned and some punishèd.**

He does not specify who, even though he asserts that he knows the Friar to be a holy man. The play ends, like so many of Shakespeare's, on a question mark, with more to be said, more to be understood, more to be forgiven; and certainly more to be punished.

At the end of THE MERCHANT OF VENICE Portia says:

> **And yet I am sure you are not satisfied**
> **Of these events at full. Let us go in**
> **And charge us there upon inter'gatories**
> **And we will answer all things faithfully.**

And at the end of MEASURE FOR MEASURE, the Duke reassures characters and audience with:

> **So bring us to our palace, where we'll show**
> **What's yet behind that's meet you all should know.**

We are not dealing with contrived and happy endings but situations in which more must be urgently questioned. Perhaps then more will be understood.

A MIDSUMMER NIGHT'S DREAM
ACT 2 SCENE 1

Oberon I know a bank where the wild thyme blows,
Where oxlips and the nodding violet grows,
Quite overcanopied with luscious woodbine,
With sweet musk-roses, and with eglantine.
There sleeps Titania sometime of the night,
Lulled in these flowers with dances and delight;
And there the snake throws her enamelled skin,
Weed wide enough to wrap a fairy in;
And with the juice of this I'll streak her eyes,
And make her full of hateful fantasies.
Take thou some of it, and seek through this grove.
A sweet Athenian lady is in love
With a disdainful youth. Anoint his eyes,
But do it when the next thing he espies
May be the lady. Thou shalt know the man
By the Athenian garments he hath on.
Effect it with some care, that he may prove
More fond on her than she upon her love;
And look thou meet me ere the first cock crow.

Puck Fear not, my lord, your servant shall do so.

A MIDSUMMER NIGHT'S DREAM
ACT 2 SCENE 1

Oberon, the King of the Fairies, is addressing his servant, Puck. Additionally and crucially, he is also addressing the audience and is telling them the next turn of the plot. He seduces them with some of the most beautiful lyrical verse in our language and then twists its beauty into 'hateful fantasies'. The play shifts from beautiful dream to hideous nightmare, from love to ungoverned ugliness and lust.

Shakespeare is too astute a dramatist to use his genius for lyric verse in a straightforward way in the theatre. He knows that the purely lyrical is usually undramatic because it is monotonous and predictable. It therefore quickly outstays its welcome. There needs to be a sub-text to it. This speech, though it is full of lovely images culled from the memory of a Warwickshire country boy, has a sick purpose. What is beautiful is turned into what is ugly. What is attractive becomes threatening.

First, the lines must be scanned. The speech begins with a monosyllabic line which is held together with the alliteration of 'bank' and 'blows'. The monosyllables would indicate that it is slow, indeed almost an incantation. At first it looks regular in its rhythm but, as explained in the discussion of scansion above, it is in fact irregular, and is followed by a completely regular iambic pentameter which reasserts the rhythm after the unexpected freedom of the first line. The pace is moved on a little also; there are no monosyllables in this second line.

The actor should now be alert to the rhymes which continue throughout the speech and contribute to the mood of hypnotic incantation. They should of course be marked but marked lightly.

Shakespeare is always very conscious of the *sound* of his lines. And these – with the assonance of '**mUSk rOSes**' and the alliteration of '**Quite**' and '**Canopied**' – are tuned to perfection. The actor should make us hear their riches – but with delicacy.

The mood changes slightly after the first four lines as Titania makes her appearance in Oberon's imaginings. The actor should notice that each line has a sound pattern that sustains it. These need relishing, but always with wit and humour. The sibilance of 'SleepS' and 'SometimeS' is counterpointed by the percussive 't's of 'TiTania' and 'some Time of the NighT'. The next line is sustained by three 'l' sounds and then by the further sibilance of 'Snake' and 'Skin'.

'Weed wide' (a Shakespearean invention), and the inversion so that the line begins with an accent and becomes a trochee rather than an iambic, gives emphasis and variety.

Oberon I know a bank where the wild thyme blows,
Where oxlips and the nodding violet grows,
Quite overcanopied with luscious woodbine,
With sweet musk-roses, and with eglantine.
There sleeps Titania sometime of the night,
Lulled in these flowers with dances and delight;
And there the snake throws her enamelled skin,
Weed wide enough to wrap a fairy in;
And with the juice of this I'll streak her eyes,
And make her full of hateful fantasies.
Take thou some of it, and seek through this grove.
A sweet Athenian lady is in love
With a disdainful youth. Anoint his eyes,
But do it when the next thing he espies
May be the lady. Thou shalt know the man
By the Athenian garments he hath on.
Effect it with some care, that he may prove
More fond on her than she upon her love;
And look thou meet me ere the first cock crow.

Puck Fear not, my lord, your servant shall do so.

The entry of the snake, 'enamelled' but threatening, adds to the sense of expectation: beauty threatens and is possibly deadly. The snake's skin is equally ambiguous. Is it a decorative garment to wrap a fairy in? Or is it a shroud?

But nothing can have prepared us for the smooth and surprising way that Oberon moves from this invocation of beauty into the next couplet, where a monosyllabic heavy line gives way to the invocation of evil and to 'hateful fantasies'. All this beauty is simply to torture his wife. The reversal is chilling but gleeful.

Oberon now moves on to the specific instructions for Puck. The lyrical writing is over and the caesura at 'disdainful youth' leads to the particular instructions for Puck. He must anoint the eyes of the young Athenian. The use of the word 'anoint' is powerful and adds to the sense of evil. Holy Emperors or Kings are anointed by the grace of God; not erring wives who are to be punished by making love to something vile. Oberon is punishing his Queen and himself. Her lust is her weakness and her punishment. His failure to be her monarch in love brings punishment to him too, though he pretends to delight in his cuckoldry.

Another caesura after 'May be the lady' indicates a further change of pace and attitude. Shakespeare doesn't need caesuras earlier in the speech, because it is a smooth, developing build, with few changes of tone. In the last six lines, we have two clear changes of tone, and thus two caesuras.

Oberon's final lines tell a complex story in an economical way using the rhythm of the verse. This young Athenian is to be more 'mad' in his love for the lady than she is in her love for the young man. Although the scansion of 'she upon her love' would be regularly,

SHE upON her LOVE

a cross-rhythm produced by a slight emphasis on the 'her' makes in clear that we are not talking about the disdainful youth but about her. The effect of the cross-rhythm may also colloquialise this regular piece of versifying.

Notice though that this cross-rhythm is not mandatory. It is a matter of choice. Providing Shakespeare's other rhythms are always present, the actor can feel, paradoxically, completely free.

The sequence ends with Oberon's last line which is monosyllabic and therefore slower and specific. It is matched by Puck. He completes the couplet and disappears with the rhyme.

HENRY IV PART ONE
ACT 2 SCENE 5

Falstaff Harry, I do not only marvel where thou spendest thy
time, but also how thou art accompanied. For though the
camomile, the more it is trodden on, the faster it grows,
yet youth, the more it is wasted the sooner it wears. That
thou art my son, I have partly thy mother's word, partly
my own opinion, but chiefly a villainous trick of thine
eye, and a foolish hanging of thy nether lip, that doth
warrant me. If then thou be son to me, here lies the
point. Why, being son to me, art thou so pointed at?
Shall the blessed son of heaven prove a micher, and eat
blackberries? A question not to be asked. Shall the son of
England prove a thief and take purses? A question to be
asked. There is a thing, Harry, which thou hast often
heard of, and it is known to many in our land by the
name of pitch. This pitch, as ancient writers do report,
doth defile. So doth the company thou keepest. For
Harry, now I do not speak to thee in drink, but in tears;
not in pleasure, but in passion; not in words only, but in
woes also. And yet there is a virtuous man whom I have
oft noted in thy company, but I know not his name.

Prince What manner of man, an it like your majesty?

Falstaff A goodly portly man i'faith, and a corpulent; of a cheerful
look, a pleasing eye, and a most noble carriage; and as I
think, his age some fifty, or by'r Lady, inclining to three
score, and now I remember me his name is Falstaff. If
that man should be lewdly given, he deceiveth me; for
Harry, I see virtue in his looks. If then the tree may be
known by the fruit, as the fruit by the tree, then
peremptorily I speak it, there is virtue in that Falstaff.
Him keep with, the rest banish.

HENRY IV PART ONE
ACT 2 SCENE 5

The prose here is deliberately formal: it enables the characters to play-act – particularly Falstaff. He is imitating Prince Hal's father, Henry IV, for the benefit of the Prince. It is beautifully tuned, but its high seriousness and analytical balance are overdone – more generous than the careful, haunted speech of the King himself. Here are ironic attempts to be both father-like and King-like. Falstaff is performing, and enjoying it. It is a dangerous scene.

The actor's first task is to find which words to point, and in prose, sense and antithesis must always be the guide.

> **Harry, I do not only marvel where thou spendest thy time,**
> **but also how thou art accompanied…**

The writing is immediately formal: 'where thou spendest thy time' is balanced by 'how thou art accompanied'. The image of the camomile is worthy of an Elizabethan sermon; and it produces a clear antithesis between 'the **faster** it **grows**' and 'the **sooner** it **wears**'. The alliteration of 'wasted' and 'wears' should lead the actor to point the words. The moralising could come out of a commonplace book. It is comically parental.

In contrast, the old joke about the mother being the only person who can be sure of the parentage of her child is slightly modified here, and leads Falstaff into a moment of affection and warmth, which belongs more to him that to the person he is imitating. Hal resembles his father because he has a villainous trick of the eye and a foolish hanging of the lower lip. The remark is personal and tender. There is love in it.

We now move into a quibble on the word 'point'. We understand 'point' in one sense – the word affirms that Harry is the legitimate son. But then why is he so 'pointed **at**' – which means commented on and accused?

A 'micher' is a truant, a drop-out. And 'blackberries' were held to be the most worthless and readily available of hedgerow fruits. So the contrast between 'the blessed son of heaven' and the wastrel who lives off the hedges like a common beggar is great. The everyday idioms of 'micher' and 'blackberries' are also part of the comic deflation.

There are of course many words in Shakespeare which are already incomprehensible. But in a large measure, if the actor understands, the audience can still understand. If the line is completely dead, then there is nothing for it but to cut it. But this should be a last resort, rarely acted on. In this instance, the sound of 'micher' and the fact that we still eat blackberries, albeit usually cultivated ones, can still make the phrase work as an anticlimax. The laugh is fairly secure.

Shall the blessed son of heaven prove a micher, and eat blackberries? **A question not to be asked.** Shall the son of England prove a thief and take purses? **A question to be asked.** There is a thing, Harry, which thou hast often heard of, and it is known to many in our land by the name of pitch. This pitch, as ancient writers do report, doth defile. So doth the company thou keepest. For Harry, now I do not speak to thee in drink, but in tears; not in pleasure, but in passion; not in words only, but in woes also. And yet there is a virtuous man whom I have oft noted in thy company, but I know not his name.

Prince **What manner of man, an it like your majesty?**

Falstaff A goodly portly man i'faith, and a corpulent; of a cheerful look, a pleasing eye, and a most noble carriage; and as I think, his age some fifty, or by'r Lady, inclining to three score, and now I remember me his name is Falstaff. If that man should be lewdly given, he deceiveth me; for Harry, I see virtue in his looks. If then the tree may be known by the fruit, as the fruit by the tree, then peremptorily I speak it, **there is virtue in that Falstaff. Him keep with, the rest banish.**

We now come to the rhetorical hinge which defines the whole speech. Lawyer-like Falstaff asks two rhetorical questions. First 'a question **not** to be asked'; then 'a question **to be** asked'. The energy that this rhetorical device produces launches Falstaff into the rest of the speech and into a mood where he dares to court danger.

He mentions his life in the underworld and the thieving which he has tempted the Prince to enjoy. In response to his challenge – 'a question to be asked' – Prince Hal says nothing.

The mock gravity of the situation leads Falstaff on to the image of 'pitch' and the observation that pitch defiles, as the Scriptures maintain. It is a further challenge to Hal to comment or even contradict. Falstaff challenges again, warning that there is a risk in the company that the Prince is keeping. Hal again says nothing. There is danger in the air.

Now Falstaff embarks on a great rhetorical build, through tears, through passion and through woes. The balances and the constant antitheses, backed by the alliteration, all need leaning on by the actor to create a concerned, moralising tone. It is like a sermon in full flow. The build finishes emotionally on 'woes also…' and this is the feed for the unexpected entrance of the virtuous man: Falstaff himself. This is Falstaff the outrageous, the mocker, the anarchist, the dangerous maker of bathos.

But his attempt to provoke Hal doesn't quite work. Hal plays the game and responds with an innocent question which is as full of mockery as Falstaff's statement. Hal's line is nearly an iambic pentameter; and providing 'An it like' is elided to one beat, the line scans:

What MANner of MAN an it LIKE your MAJesTY;

the sudden change into near-verse increases the atmosphere of danger; and the alliteration with all the 'm's adds to the mock naïvety, the assumed innocence.

Falstaff now supplies a courtly prose portrait of himself. He manages, after feigning forgetfulness, to remember his own name. This passage is of course an eloquent means of preparing for the crucial development of the plot. Falstaff knows he cannot stay forever by the side of his Prince. The Prince knows it too; and the original audience, steeped in the divinity of royalty, must have felt the precariousness of the relationship even more than modern audiences. Here it is deliberately focused with the emotive

HENRY IV PART ONE, Royal Shakespeare Company 1964.
Ian Holm as Prince Hal and Hugh Griffith as Falstaff.

word 'banish'. Falstaff advises that all the Eastcheap friends except him should be got rid of; it is a challenge for the future and every one – Prince Hal, Falstaff and the audience – knows that it will not be met. It can't be. From this moment, we know in our hearts where the play is going.

The artificiality of the language and its considered rhythms have enabled prince and surrogate parent to act out and express the whole danger of the situation – present and future. In verse, it would be less artificial and ultimately less dangerous. This is a formal charade that we will remember through two plays until Falstaff is banished indeed.

JULIUS CAESAR
ACT 3 SCENE 2

Brutus　Be patient till the last.
Romans, countrymen, and lovers, hear me for my
cause and be silent that you may hear. Believe
me for mine honour, and have respect to mine
honour, that you may believe. Censure me in your
wisdom, and awake your senses that you may the
better judge. If there be any in this assembly,
any dear friend of Caesar's, to him I say that
Brutus' love to Caesar was no less than his. If
then that friend demand why Brutus rose against
Caesar, this is my answer: not that I loved
Caesar less, but that I loved Rome more. Had you
rather Caesar were living, and die all slaves,
than that Caesar were dead, to live all free men?
As Caesar loved me I weep for him; as he was
fortunate I rejoice at it; as he was valiant I
honour him; but as he was ambitious I slew him.
There is tears for his love; joy for his fortune;
honour for his valour; and death for his ambition.
Who is here so base that would be a bondman? If
any speak, for him have I offended. Who is here
so rude that would not be a Roman? If any speak,
for him I have offended. Who is here so vile,
that will not love his country? If any speak, for
him have I offended. I pause for a reply.

All　None Brutus none.

Brutus　Then none have I offended. I have done no more to
Caesar than you shall do to Brutus.

JULIUS CAESAR
ACT 3 SCENE 2

Brutus ascends the pulpit and thus claims the right to speak to the people. His duty is to explain the murder of Caesar – why the conspirators did it, and how they did it.

Before Brutus begins the formal oration, there is a three beat iambic line followed by a pause. This is a moment of ordinary speech – in modern parlance 'Be patient till the last' means 'Hear me out', 'Let me finish'. It is the preparation for something formal and considered.

What follows is a carefully thought out and almost clinically constructed piece of public speaking. Its discipline and its refusal to be emotional, its restraint and its even-handedness are all in sharp contrast to what is to follow – Mark Antony speaking free verse which is emotional, direct, spontaneous and apparently without any hidden purpose at all. Retrospectively we shall see that Brutus, although he looks calculating with his careful prose, was in fact striving to be honest. Mark Antony, on the other hand, was using his candour and his apparent honesty to be very manipulative. But then Mark Antony is a great spontaneous public speaker, and Brutus is not. So here the prose is performing a major dramatic function which could not easily be achieved any other way.

First, it has an insistent beat – not regular because this is the prose of contrast and of antithetical thought. But nonetheless it has a rhythm which the actor should lean on. Brutus asks to be *heard* for his *cause* and that they should be *silent* that they may *hear*. He asks that they will respect his honour and therefore believe him. This is the formal preamble.

Now comes the paradox that gives the theme to the speech. Brutus the murderer states categorically that no-one loved Caesar more than him. But Brutus, much as he loved Caesar, loved Rome more. And that is his case. The constant balances of 'less' with 'more'; of 'living' with 'dead'; of 'slaves' with 'free men'; the antithesis between 'loving' and 'weeping' – all lead up to the shocking surprise: that because he was *ambitious*, Brutus *slew* him; that was the reason for Caesar's death.

All these contrasts try to justify a monstrous crime. But they are not crowd-pleasers like Mark Antony's are going to be; they are rather the masterly paradoxes of the rhetorician. They might appeal to the Senators, as Cicero appealed to them. But they are too cold for the common people.

JULIUS CAESAR, Royal Shakespeare Company 1995.
John Nettles as Brutus and Julian Glover as Cassius.

Brutus having, as he thinks, been honest now uses the rhetorical device of asking anyone who has been offended by him to speak. In question after question, he invites interruption. To our surprise he has won them over – but grudgingly. They are impressed by his rhetorical skill, but only partially convinced. Their minds respect him, but not their hearts. The stage is now set for the colloquial verse of Mark Antony to be more persuasive than the public speaker.

Acting this speech by Brutus requires a sober delight in paradox and balance, in climax and hyperbole. Brutus can be, and indeed is, very emotional. But his emotions are restrained by the disciplines of his careful balanced speaking. He does not let go, as Mark Antony does. He does not use his emotions.

Shakespeare's dramatic use of rhetoric is here masterly. He knows precisely what effect he's making, and only prose and the tradition of rhetorical disputation could achieve it. Once again though, Shakespeare is using the form, not in a pure but in an ambiguous sense. Just as lyric verse is usually to be interpreted critically because it springs in some measure from self-indulgence, so, here, pure rhetoric is shown deficient in humanity.

TWELFTH NIGHT
ACT 1 SCENE 1

Orsino If music be the food of love, play on,
Give me excess of it, that surfeiting,
The appetite may sicken and so die.
That strain again, it had a dying fall.
O it came o'er my ear like the sweet sound
That breathes upon a bank of violets,
Stealing and giving odour. Enough, no more,
'Tis not so sweet now as it was before.
(*music ceases*)
O spirit of love, how quick and fresh art thou,
That notwithstanding thy capacity
Receiveth as the sea, naught enters there,
Of what validity and pitch so e'er
But falls into abatement and low price
Even in a minute! So full of shapes is fancy
That it alone is high fantastical.

Curio Will you go hunt, my lord?

Orsino   What, Curio?

Curio   The hart.

Orsino Why so I do, the noblest that I have.
O, when mine eyes did see Olivia first
Methought she purged the air of pestilence;
That instant was I turned into a hart,
And my desires, like fell and cruel hounds,
E'er since pursue me.

TWELFTH NIGHT
ACT 1 SCENE 1

The Folio gives no stage directions about music, but clearly music is playing: the Duke Orsino is asking for it to continue:

If music be the food of love, play on

This is a perfectly regular iambic line. It sets the mood of the scene that will show us a sensualist who is in love with love, and perhaps even more in love with himself and his own changeable moods than he is with the lady of his choice.

'Music' is the most important word in the line – it is indeed capitalised in the Folio, as is 'love'. This points up the antithesis between 'music' and 'love', and is the beginning of an extraordinarily mixed metaphor which involves all the senses. Once music has been transformed into the food which sustains love (with all the associations of appetite and satiation) it must 'play on' and be indulged more and more. It is an addiction. We are immediately in a world of deep sensuality. The line scans perfectly. The paradox is the mixed metaphor. Music is food, not melody.

The second line begins with an inversion:

Give me excess of it, that surfeiting

The even musicality of the first line is challenged by this inversion. This trochee (DUM-di) is again a favourite device. It surprises the audience and it breaks the hypnotic regularity of the iambics. New energy is given to the incoming line. The actor should of course point the active word 'GIVE'.

The line develops the sensuality by the sibilant 'S's in 'eXCeSS' and 'Surfeiting'. 'Surfeiting' is to run the risk of making yourself sick, of over-indulging. The line has the necessary phrase break at the end of it and should not be run on:

Give me excess of it, that surfeiting…

an upward inflection on this slight hesitation creates expectation and should make us ask 'What does surfeiting give us'? What happens when we 'surfeit'? Once again Shakespeare's phrasing is built on the end of the lines: that is where the main weight of meaning is to be found. It is therefore almost never the place to hurry on to the next line. The end of the line gives a slight lift in energy, an expectation, so that preparation can be made for the next phrase. It is not a stop. It punctuates lightly, arouses

If music be the food of love, play on,
Give me excess of it, that surfeiting,
The appetite may sicken and so die.
That strain again, it had a dying fall.
O it came o'er my ear like the sweet sound
That breathes upon a bank of violets,
Stealing and giving odour. Enough, no more,
'Tis not so sweet now as it was before.

expectation, and leads us to the next statement. So what will happen to us if we 'surfeit'? And here comes the answer to the question:

The appetite may sicken and so die.

Sibilance again with 'Sicken' and 'So'. And the word 'appetite' is at last spoken. Hunger and sex are equated. And the word 'die' brings us to a conclusion. It is a witty conclusion, an end as well as a beginning, and Orsino knows it. 'Die' is the Elizabethan word for orgasm. It is the longed-for finish. Satiation.

The modern actor may very well hesitate after 'sicken', but the smoothness of the line needs to flow on: the appetite is 'sickening' until it dies. No break is necessary – indeed it is destructive. The antithesis between 'sicken' and 'die' (because the one produces the other) is clearer if the line is kept intact.

The music continues to play. Indeed, there should be a pause in the speech after 'die' to allow Orsino to listen to it. A pause is always possible at the end of a line if it makes dramatic, formal or musical sense.

The particularly mellifluous nature of Orsino's verse should remind the actor of another rule: breath should only be taken at the end of the line. To rush on to the next line, particularly when the phrases are full of metaphors (which the character is supposed to be inventing) is to sell the audience short and confuse them. So having paused and listened to the music, Orsino comments:

That strain again, it had a dying fall.

It is a clear interruption of the music, a command to repeat what has just been played, which the musicians obviously obey. A 'strain' is a shape of notes, a phrase of melody. But there are rich paradoxes here because the word has many other meanings and associations, and actor and audience can be alive to them. The word stands for a strong impulse of high emotion; it is also a particular tendency or disposition. As a verb it means to force or constrain, to exceed bounds, to find difficult. It is clearly a deliberate word of tension. The particular reason that Orsino is envious of it at this moment is that the 'strain' has a 'dying fall' – that is, a downward musical cadence which is sad and conclusive. This term is also complex. It can mean the downward stroke of the sword, the fall at low ebb tide, or the end of a bout of wrestling. But the qualifying word 'dying' is the significant one. The actor should remember again that 'die' in Elizabethan

O it came o'er my ear like the sweet sound
That breathes upon a bank of violets,
Stealing and giving odour. Enough, no more,
'Tis not so sweet now as it was before.

slang is when the lover reaches orgasm. So the line falls away, concluding like the satisfied lover. And that which is 'fallen' is no longer standing.

Orsino savours the phrase again. He is amused by the paradoxes even at the moment that love is hurting him. He listens to the music and speaks over it, telling his Court:

> O it came o'er my ear like the sweet sound
> That breathes upon a bank of violets,
> Stealing and giving odour. Enough, no more,
> 'Tis not so sweet now as it was before.

A great deal is going on here and the text is full of signals for the actor. The repeat of the musical phrase earns this heavily sensual tribute. Orsino is remembering it as it was, describing it as it is repeated. He is indeed being reckless in remembering the pleasure of an experience at the very moment that he repeats it. Most sexual experiences don't bear repetition immediately after they have been savoured. But first, he expresses his pleasure by the mixed metaphors: there is a **sound** that **breathes** on violets, that **takes away** and yet **gives odour**. It is a giving and a taking expressed in a sensual contradiction worthy of John Donne. Notice also the assonance of:

> O it came O'ER my EAR like the Sweet Sound...

The 'o's' and 'r's' and 's's' express Orsino's orgasmic state. The rich assonance of the 'r' sounds ('o'er' and 'ear') are especially potent.

Several editors have suggested the substitution of 'south' instead of 'sound' – so that the metaphor shall not be so wildly mixed. But surely this riot of contradictory senses is the point of the passage. Lovers all like describing their moods, and Orsino appropriates everything sensuous in an attempt to define his obsessive sensuality. Shakespeare can often suffer from his correctors.

The elision of 'over' to 'o'er' gives us a weighty monosyllabic line again. And if the actor keeps to the regular iambic rhythm, it produces a strange mis-scansion because the accent falls on 'the'. He has to elide 'like' and 'the' colloquially so that the emphasis lands on **'sweet'** and **'sound'**. This, with the alliteration added, makes the two words concrete and particular.

O it came o'er my ear like the sweet sound
That breathes upon a bank of violets,
Stealing and giving odour. Enough, no more,
'Tis not so sweet now as it was before.
(*music ceases*)
O spirit of love, how quick and fresh art thou,
That notwithstanding thy capacity
Receiveth as the sea, naught enters there,
Of what validity and pitch so e'er
But falls into abatement and low price
Even in a minute! So full of shapes is fancy
That it alone is high fantastical.

Now comes another significant point: we meet our first caesura (the stop in the middle of a line) in the play. But even when there is a full stop, the sanctity of the whole line must be preserved. The actor needs to change pace at the end of the previous line so that the first half of the new line can be slowed up in order to earn the time for the full stop. The slowing up of course needs motivating. It seems here that at the very moment of his sexual satisfaction, Orsino is suddenly overcome with disappointment and wilfully rejects the whole experience. It is the first sign of his unpredictable temperament. A scene that begins as great lyric poetry ends by expressing the dreadful loneliness that comes to the self-indulgent after love, whether the love be real or imagined. Here it is written out:

> **O it came o'er my ear like the sweet sound**
> **That breathes upon a bank of violets**

Orsino is now at the point of ecstasy, the tempo changes and becomes slower, heavier and even more sensual:

> **Stealing and giving odour.**

Here there is a break – but not sufficient to wreck the line, only to earn the full stop. Here is the rejection. Perhaps Orsino now realises that he is only imagining, not experiencing, this lovemaking. And so the rhyme and the change of attitude show the depth of disappointment and frustration.

> **Enough, no more.**
> **'Tis not so sweet now as it was before.**

The rhyme emphasises explanation and disappointment. And the music has finally produced a totally unsatisfactory experience. Orsino is more lonely, more miserable than he was before. Music is no substitute for his lady; and finally it is an irritant rather than a medicine to his passion. So the music stops.

Note the elision of '**spirit**' in '**O spirit of love**' to make the line scan. It needs pronouncing as one syllable rather than two. '**Capacity**' at the end of the next line is like the earlier '**surfeiting**' – an end-of-line herald to announce what is to come. Here it sets up the image of the sea, the bringer and taker of life. The unexpected rhyme ('**there**' and '**e'er**') at the end of the line increases the mystery of the sea and its power of destruction.

TWELFTH NIGHT, Royal Shakespeare Company 1960.
Derek Godfrey as Orsino.

The caesura change of pace on '**Even in a minute!**' enables Orsino to muse on the power of the imagination in love ('**Fancy**'). He pays ironic tribute to the changeable power of love: it alone can change with the speed of light.

There can now be a beat, a hiatus where, with the music silenced, Orsino's Court wonders what is to happen next.

Curio suggests hunting and his suggestion must be paced so that his two speeches and Orsino's reply make one line. The changeable Orsino puns on the word 'hart'.

The actor should point the naming of a principal character with the word '**Olivia**' and notice that the assonance with the '**O**' at the beginning of the line sets up its importance. The alliteration on '**purged**' and '**pestilence**' helps the extravagance of the hyperbole and needs marking. Everything sick and dangerous – the plague itself – was purged by the beauty of this woman. Orsino then sees himself as a hart to be hunted and killed by his own desire. It is a self-inflicted torture. The madness of love has been well established.

TWELFTH NIGHT
ACT 1 SCENE 5

Viola   Good madam, let me see your face.

Olivia   Have you any commission from your lord to negotiate
with my face? You are now out of your text. But we
will draw the curtain and show you the picture (*she
unveils*). Look you sir, such a one I was this present.
Is't not well done?

Viola   Excellently done, if God did all.

Olivia   'Tis in grain, sir, 'twill endure wind and weather.

Viola   'Tis beauty truly blent, whose red and white
Nature's own sweet and cunning hand laid on.
Lady you are the cruellest she alive
If you will lead these graces to the grave
And leave the world no copy.

Olivia   O sir, I will not be so hard-hearted. I will give out
divers schedules of my beauty. It shall be inventoried
and every particle and utensil labelled to my will, as
item two lips indifferent red; *item* two gray eyes with
lids to them; *item* one neck, one chin, and so forth.
Were you sent hither to praise me?

Viola   I see you what you are, you are too proud,
But if you were the devil, you are fair.
My lord and master loves you. O such love
Could but be recompensed though you were crowned
The nonpareil of beauty.

Olivia   How does he love me?

Viola   With adorations, fertile tears,
With groans that thunder love, with sighs of fire.

Olivia   Your lord does know my mind, I cannot love him.
Yet I suppose him virtuous, know him noble,
Of great estate, of fresh and stainless youth,
In voices well divulged, free, learn'd, and valiant,
And in dimension and the shape of nature
A gracious person, yet I cannot love him.
He might have took his answer long ago.

Viola   If I did love you in my master's flame
With such a suffering, such a deadly life,

In your denial I would find no sense,
I would not understand it.

Olivia   Why, what would you?

Viola Make me a willow cabin at your gate
And call upon my soul within the house,
Write loyal cantons of contemnèd love,
And sing them loud even in the dead of night;
Halloo your name to the reverberate hills,
And make the babbling gossip of the air
Cry out 'Olivia!' O you should not rest
Between the elements of air and earth
But you should pity me.

Olivia   You might do much.
What is your parentage?

Viola Above my fortunes, yet my state is well.
I am a gentleman.

Olivia   Get you to your lord.
I cannot love him. Let him send no more,
Unless perchance, you come to me again
To tell me how he takes it. Fare you well.
I thank you for your pains. Spend this for me.

Viola I am no fee'd post, lady, keep your purse.
My master not myself lacks recompense.
Love make his heart of flint that you shall love,
And let your fervour like my master's be
Placed in contempt. Farewell, fair cruelty.

Viola Good madam, let me see your face.

Olivia Have you any commission from your lord to negotiate
with my face? You are now out of your text. But we
will draw the curtain and show you the picture (*she
unveils*). **Look you sir, such a one I was this present.**
Is't not well done?

Viola **Excellently done, if God did all.**

Olivia 'Tis in grain, sir, 'twill endure wind and weather.

Viola 'Tis beauty truly blent, whose red and white
Nature's own sweet and cunning hand laid on.
Lady you are the cruellest she alive
If you will lead these graces to the grave
And leave the world no copy.

TWELFTH NIGHT
ACT 1 SCENE 5

Viola, a girl disguised as a boy, goes as Duke Orsino's page to the Lady Olivia in an attempt to advance Orsino's protestations of love. She is herself already secretly in love with the Duke. During the course of this scene in which comedy is laced with heartbreak, Olivia falls in love with the page. Meanwhile, the page, in the person of Viola, has the painful task of wooing a woman on behalf of the man she loves herself.

One of the themes of TWELFTH NIGHT is the uncontrollable madness of love. In this scene, we see Olivia's love for the page growing before our eyes. In the meantime, Viola, honourable as ever, becomes emotional on behalf of the Duke, partly to avoid her own jealousy, partly as a transference of her passion. But by being honourable, she makes things worse. Shakespeare needs every technical device available in order to show the difference between uncontrollable passion and controllable reason – which is nonetheless controlled with difficulty. The tension of the scene is therefore built on the sudden transitions from prose into verse and from verse back into prose. The actor must be very aware of these changes and find ways of using them. They always signal a fundamental change of attitude. Verse is about feeling and anguish leading to protest; prose is about reason, argument and wit.

Olivia is veiled, so Viola, in a line of verse, asks her to reveal herself. The line only has four feet – which would indicate that there is a slight written-in pause before Olivia continues in prose. One of the techniques of the scene is the tendency of the prose, under the emotional stress of the situation, to develop iambic rhythms which almost transform it into blank verse. Time and again, feelings take off and fly into verse or near-verse. It is the perfect way to chart the febrile nature of the encounter.

As Olivia unveils, she almost speaks in verse:

Look you sir, such a one I was this present.

Viola answers with another four-foot iambic which takes her honesty perilously near to bitchiness. Is this unthinking candour or a woman being jealous about another woman? The audience should not be sure.

Olivia counters by pulling the text firmly back towards prose. But Viola, aware of her duty to the Duke and the need to convince Olivia of his passion, breaks into fervent, though conventional, verse, using the forms of love poetry and the age-old argument of the lover to his mistress: she must not die before she has left the world a copy of herself. It is her duty to pass on her beauty – that is, have his child.

Olivia O sir, I will not be so hard-hearted. I will give out
divers schedules of my beauty. It shall be inventoried
and every particle and utensil labelled to my will, as
item two lips indifferent red; *item* two gray eyes with
lids to them; *item* one neck, one chin, and so forth.
Were you sent hither to praise me?

Viola I see you what you are, you are too proud.
But if you were the devil, you are fair.
My lord and master loves you. O such love
Could but be recompensed though you were crowned
The nonpareil of beauty.

Olivia   How does he love me?

Viola With adorations, fertile tears,
With groans that thunder love, with sighs of fire.

Olivia Your lord does know my mind, I cannot love him.
Yet I suppose him virtuous, know him noble,
Of great estate, of fresh and stainless youth,
In voices well divulged, free, learn'd and valiant
And in dimension and the shape of nature
A gracious person, yet I cannot love him.
He might have took his answer long ago.

Olivia mocks this courtly outburst with dry and witty prose. She suggests that her beauty shall be catalogued – '**inventoried**' – so that future generations may know how she looked. The child is unnecessary. Viola is reduced to silence. Olivia has to ask, '**Were you sent hither to praise me?**' Again Viola moves from prose back into verse. But it is a verse with a difference. Here is a classic, simple, monosyllabic Shakespearean line without frills or furbelows, and it comes from the bottom of the heart. Shakespeare's most passionate outbursts are often couched in plain, simple speech. She admits that Olivia is beautiful, but nonetheless accuses her of pride.

The caesura break allows for the two slow phrases of sincerity which surround it, while the repetition of '**loves**' and '**love**' shows the depths of Viola's emotion. The word '**love**' at the end of the line demands the usual slight hesitation of energy, the usual slight pedal break. But this is no ordinary love. This love is so supreme that it is at the end of the line; and the emphasis turns it into an hyperbole. The three 'C's of '**Could**' '**reCompense**' and '**Crowned**' give a percussive pain to the line. Viola's honesty makes her balance her master's passion with his mistress's beauty.

There is a change of tempo which relates to the caesura. '**Crowned**' is the end of the line and heralds a change of pace so that

> ### The nonpareil of beauty.
> #### How does he love me?

allows Olivia to invite the attractive young page to continue his love speeches. Olivia is no dutiful mourner of her dead brother, but a young lady who enjoys flirting. And she wants this attractive young page to go on making his love speeches.

Viola is disconcerted for a moment and has to fall back again on the clichés of courtly love. Her first line has the hesitancy of a four-beat line as opposed to a five-beat line. Possibly there is a small pause after '**tears**' while she gathers herself for the onslaught of the next line, with its hyperboles of '**thunder**' that '**groans**' and '**fire**' that '**sighs**'.

This is not sincere feeling though; it is overstated stuff, trying to make its case. And Olivia deals with it smartly by making the next seven lines a complete deflation of the Duke and his love suit. For the first time, however, she speaks in verse; and although it is precise and practical, it allows the heat of the scene to be maintained. Viola's anguish is about to deliver a heartfelt assessment of the pain of love. It would be too big an emotional jump to go from prose straight back into this verse.

Olivia Your lord does know my mind, I cannot love him.
Yet I suppose him virtuous, know him noble,
Of great estate, of fresh and stainless youth,
In voices well divulged, free, learn'd, and valiant,
And in dimension and the shape of nature
A gracious person, yet **I cannot love him.**
He might have took his answer long ago.

Viola If I did love you in my master's flame
With such a suffering, such a deadly life,
In your denial I would find no sense,
I would not understand it.

Olivia   Why, what would you?

Viola **Make me a willow cabin at your gate**
And call upon my soul within the house,
Write loyal cantons of contemnèd love,
And sing them loud even in the dead of night;
Halloo your name to the reverberate hills,
And make the babbling gossip of the air
Cry out 'Olivia!' O you should not rest
Between the elements of air and earth
But you should pity me.

Olivia   **You might do much.**
What is your parentage?

In the meantime, Olivia sustains the heat by being factual and heartless. She seemingly has no compassion. The seven lines express the unthinking cruelty, even contempt, that one who cannot return love feels towards the one who offers it.

I cannot love him.
He might have took his answer long ago.

Viola is appalled and yet provoked. She knows how Orsino suffers for Olivia; it is perhaps near the suffering that she endures for him. Her reply is simple, heartfelt and direct. Yet she invokes a string of unforgettable images. There are no clichés of love here: just a sincerity which goes straight to the heart of the matter – and to the heart of Olivia. Viola's next speech contains the alliteration of '**Such**' and '**Suffering**'; and the repeated '**such**' delivers the mordant quibble on '**deadly life**' – deadly in that it produces death, and so obliterates life. But by the time Viola gets to 'I would not understand it', Olivia can complete the line and (entranced as she is) make a simple invitation to Viola to launch into a love speech which contains none of the conventional sighing and groaning, none of the hyperboles of '**thundering**', but is an unforgettable series of images about the pangs of despised love, forged at this moment in the white heat of emotion.

The willow cabin is by the gate. The watcher (who is also the carer) cries out her name to '**the reverberate hills**' because he is denied her. The willow is a sign of unrequited love, and the lover will keep eternal watch in the cabin at the gate of the lady he loves. He will call upon her, sing to her, '**halloo her name**', like a chorus of celebrating huntsmen. Finally, all the sounds of the air will cry out in unison '**Olivia**'.

This half-line is the climax of the speech. The second half-line modulates into a mood that is more exhausted, post-coital and controlled. The further half-lines after the speech make up the usual unit. '**But you should pity me**' slows down a great deal, so that Olivia can complete *on cue* with:

You might do much.

The cue must be directly taken. The audience then realise that Olivia has fallen in love.

I have an edition in front of me which says of the Willow Cabin speech: 'this passage was probably spoken by the actor with emphasis and energy as a kind of show piece'. This is the exact opposite of the dramatic truth. Viola is not showing off: she is

Viola Make me a willow cabin at your gate
And call upon my soul within the house,
Write loyal cantons of contemnèd love,
And sing them loud even in the dead of night;
Halloo your name to the reverberate hills,
And make the babbling gossip of the air
Cry out 'Olivia!' O you should not rest
Between the elements of air and earth
But you should pity me.

Olivia **You might do much.**
What is your parentage?

Viola Above my fortunes, yet my state is well.
I am a gentleman.

Olivia   Get you to your lord.
I cannot love him. Let him send no more
Unless perchance, you come to me again
To tell me how he takes it. Fare you well.
I thank you for your pains. Spend this for me.

Viola I am no fee'd post, lady, keep your purse.
My master not myself lacks recompense.
Love make his heart of flint that you shall love,
And let your fervour like my master's be
Placed in contempt. Farewell, fair cruelty.

demonstrating and suffering the power of love – her love for Orsino. Even worse, this edition goes on to state, 'the short line at the end may indicate a pause before Olivia replies'. There is no pause. There is a half-line so that Olivia can complete the line on cue. Properly timed, without a pause, Olivia's line gets in performance a warm laugh of understanding. The audience have watched Olivia fall in love with a young man whom they know to be a girl. Shakespeare does not carefully construct his texts with answering half-lines expecting them to be surrounded by pauses.

It has to be said, though, that this particular moment presents fascinating problems. There are not two half-lines here, but three:

> But you should pity me.
> You might do much.
> What is your parentage?

It is impossible to tell from the Folio which half-line connects with which. It is perfectly possible for instance for '**You might do much**' to be the first half of a line which is completed by '**What is your parentage?**' The pause would then come after Viola's half-line.

I have tried this in performance and found it predictable, somewhat sentimental and never getting a response from the audience. So I prefer the first solution. Olivia then takes a half-line pause before 'What is your parentage?' in order to collect herself and continue her examination of this fascinating young man.

Olivia therefore asks about the boy's parentage. Viola replies with care because she is dissembling. As a general remark (and trying not to lie too much), she says slowly that she is a gentleman. Her brother was a gentleman; so was her father. Her social standing is correct but not her sex. Notice that her slowness allows Olivia to complete the line. The fact that this page is a gentleman means that Olivia may be able to pursue her passion. This page is not necessarily beneath her. If he is a gentleman, he may be a young courtier. She has found love and might be able to marry the page, and to deny the Duke once and for all.

Olivia is now in a state. The pace is therefore constantly changed so that the actor can maintain the line. But these changes show that Olivia is very flustered. And that is clearly why Shakespeare has written this sudden rash of caesuras.

TWELFTH NIGHT, Stratford-upon-Avon 1958.
Dorothy Tutin as Viola and Geraldine McEwan as Olivia.

There is a beautiful lame excuse when, having asked the page to come again, there is a change of pace on the end of the line while Olivia invents an explanation:

To tell me how he takes it.

Olivia then makes the mistake of offering a tip. This enrages Viola and presumably makes this untypical page even more attractive. She remembers herself sufficiently to bring the business back to Orsino's love. She is going home empty-handed, without any recompense for her master. So she says in some heat (again a very untypical page) that when Olivia loves, she hopes that her fervour, like Orsino's, will be rejected.

There is then a rhyme to give her a strong exit, and the personification of Olivia as Cruelty finishes the scene. Viola's integrity has been sorely tested, but has survived. And Olivia is in love.

HAMLET
ACT 3 SCENE 3

Claudius O my offence is rank, it smells to heaven.
It hath the primal eldest curse upon't,
A brother's murder. Pray can I not,
Though inclination be as sharp as will,
My stronger guilt defeats my strong intent,
And like a man to double business bound,
I stand in pause where I shall first begin,
And both neglect. What if this cursèd hand
Were thicker than itself with brother's blood,
Is there not rain enough in the sweet heavens
To wash it white as snow? Whereto serves mercy
But to confront the visage of offence?
And what's in prayer but this twofold force,
To be forestallèd ere we come to fall,
Or pardoned being down? Then I'll look up,
My fault is past – but O, what form of prayer
Can serve my turn? 'Forgive me my foul murder'?
That cannot be, since I am still possessed
Of those effects for which I did the murder –
My crown, mine own ambition, and my queen.
May one be pardoned and retain th'offence?
In the corrupted currents of this world
Offence's gilded hand may shove by justice,
And oft 'tis seen the wicked prize itself
Buys out the law. But 'tis not so above.
There is no shuffling, there the action lies
In his true nature, and we ourselves compelled
Even to the teeth and forehead of our faults
To give in evidence. What then? What rests?
Try what repentance can. What can it not?
Yet what can it when one cannot repent?
O wretched state, O bosom black as death,
O limèd soul, that struggling to be free,
Art more engaged! Help, angels! Make assay.
Bow stubborn knees; and heart with strings of steel
Be soft as sinews of the new born babe.
All may be well.
(he kneels. Enter Hamlet)

Hamlet Now might I do it pat, now he is praying.
And now I'll do't; and so he goes to heaven,
And so am I revenged. That would be scanned.
A villain kills my father, and for that
I, his sole son, do this same villain send
To heaven.
O this is hire and salary, not revenge!
He took my father grossly, full of bread,
With all his crimes broad blown, as flush as May;
And how his audit stands, who knows save heaven?
But in our circumstance and course of thought
'Tis heavy with him. And am I then revenged
To take him in the purging of his soul,
When he is fit and seasoned for his passage?
No.
Up sword, and know thou a more horrid hint.
When he is drunk asleep, or in his rage,
Or in th'incestuous pleasure of his bed,
At gaming, swearing, or about some act
That has no relish of salvation in't,
Then trip him that his heels may kick at heaven,
And that his soul may be as damned and black
As hell whereto it goes. My mother stays,
This physic but prolongs thy sickly days.

Claudius My words fly up, my thoughts remain below.
Words without thoughts never to heaven go.

Claudius O my offence is rank, it smells to heaven.
It hath the primal eldest curse upon't,
A brother's murder. Pray can I not,
Though inclination be as sharp as will,
My stronger guilt defeats my strong intent,
And like a man to double business bound,
I stand in pause where I shall first begin,
And both neglect.

HAMLET
ACT 3 SCENE 3

Claudius is trying to pray, unsuccessfully. The first line is a clear confession: his crime stinks to heaven. If we needed any confirmation of his guilt, we have it now. The mask is off.

Crucially though, Claudius is speaking not to himself, but to the audience. It is his confession to us. His guilt is intense, as intense as his need for prayer. Yet he knows that he is damned – and so he is incapable of prayer. And this emphasises that he is trapped in the consequences of what he has done.

The offence that smells to heaven is an image that is deliberately disgusting. Shakespeare is not refined. He has no constraining poetic diction: the whole of the English language is his, beautiful or ugly, sensual or revolting. This is not heroic verse, but an absolute demonstration of the cancer that is eating Claudius. He is telling it as it is. Then Claudius leads us on to God's curse and then to Cain and Abel. He is dealing with a brother's murder.

The complete confession comes at the beginning of the third line. And the subsequent caesura on the full stop means that the tempo of the first half of the line – the confession – has to have a pace that allows for the full stop. '**A brother's murder**' is therefore properly isolated. There is additionally an irregularity in the scansion in the caesura line which could lead the actor to choose a highly emotional delivery, fighting for control: it is a terrible curse, not to be able to pray. The irregularity of the line (it has only four feet) supports this interpretation.

a BROTHer's MURder. PRAY can I NOT...

It is followed by a completely regular line in which it seems as if Claudius regains control. He points the antithesis between 'guilt' and 'intent'. The neurotic contradictions which are destroying Claudius are clearly defined.

The subsequent regular verse controls his emotions a little and a further use of antitheses ('**pause**' balanced by '**begin**', and then the paradox of '**both neglect**') takes us to the next caesura.

Claudius' emotional control is challenged again in the next three and a half lines. The cursed hand is imagined to be thicker than itself because it is caked with brother's blood. The antithesis reminds us of MACBETH. The emotion that is released by this image drives Claudius to the invocation of the heavens and the longing for a purity which should be white as snow.

What if this cursèd hand
Were thicker than itself with brother's blood,
Is there not rain enough in the sweet heavens
To wash it white as snow? Whereto serves mercy
But to confront the visage of offence?
And what's in prayer but this twofold force,
To be forestallèd ere we come to fall,
Or pardoned being down? Then I'll look up,
My fault is past – but O, what form of prayer
Can serve my turn? 'Forgive me my foul murder'?
That cannot be, since I am still possessed
Of those effects for which I did the murder –
My crown, mine own ambition, and my queen.
May one be pardoned and retain th'offence?
In the corrupted currents of this world
Offence's gilded hand may shove by justice,
And oft 'tis seen the wicked prize itself
Buys out the law. But 'tis not so above.

The actor should be alert to the weight at the end of the lines and that they almost always contain the key words – '**hand**', '**blood**', '**heavens**', '**mercy**', '**offence**'. These are the words that need pointing. There is a powerful antithesis between '**cursèd hand**' and '**brother's blood**'. The pace quickens up as Claudius invokes '**mercy**' and the end of the line delivers the next metaphysical thought: mercy has no potency unless it confronts the offence face to face.

The sense is now becoming as knotted as Claudius' mind. The actor must lead the audience clearly through these tortured thoughts. The paradox of prayer is that it both saves us from temptation and rescues us if we have sinned: 'Lead us not into temptation, but deliver us from evil.'

Mercy seen as rain that washes away sin recalls THE MERCHANT OF VENICE:

> The quality of mercy is not strained.
> It droppeth as the gentle rain from heaven
> Upon the place beneath. It is twice blessed:
> It blesseth him that gives and him that takes.

This twofold force of prayer leads the audience to set aside the Old Testament and consider the compassion and forgiveness of the New Testament. It also serves to highlight the religious terror that is stalking Claudius. In this soliloquy, he is constantly struggling for redemption. When he fails to find it, he becomes for the rest of the play a figure wholly possessed by evil. This scene is his turning point and the play's.

There is alliteration here which guides the actor to emphasise slightly the word: '**conFront**', '**oFFence**', '**twoFold**', '**Force**', '**Forestallèd**', '**Fall**'. The repeated questioning and Claudius' emotional insecurity are again supported and expressed by the constant changes of pace called for by the caesuras.

Now comes the key moral question:

> May one be pardoned and retain th'offence?

Claudius is a realist. He knows that in this corrupt world (notice the alliteration) the hand of the sinner bearing a bribe of gold can surmount justice; indeed it can often bribe the law. The simplicity of the antithesis when this profoundly frightened man tells the audience '**But 'tis not so above**' shows eloquently where his need for prayer is coming from. The caesura break between '**law**' and '**But**' sets up the whole haunted line.

There is no shuffling, there the action lies
In his true nature, and we ourselves compelled
Even to the teeth and forehead of our faults
To give in evidence. What then? What rests?
Try what repentance can. What can it not?
Yet what can it when one cannot repent?
O wretched state, O bosom black as death,
O limèd soul, that struggling to be free,
Art more engaged! Help, angels! Make assay.
Bow, stubborn knees; and heart with strings of steel
Be soft as sinews of the new born babe.
All may be well.
(*he kneels. Enter Hamlet*)

We now plunge further into tortured speech. The surprising use of the word '**shuffling**' (a colloquial term from the world of conmen, meaning evasion); the end of the next line on '**compelled**', setting up a sense of expectation which delivers the almost surrealistic line:

> Even to the teeth and forehead of our faults

all show the tension which is destroying him. It is a most tortured way of saying 'face to face'. The alliteration of '**forehead**' and '**faults**' adds to the disgust. The teeth are predatory: our sins destroy us like ravening wolves.

The scansion of the two lines

> Try what repentance can. What can it not?
> Yet what can it when one cannot repent?

is a rhetorical device which precisely defines the dilemma. The scansion makes it clear:

> TRY what rePENtance CAN. What CAN it NOT?
> Yet WHAT can IT when ONE canNOT repENT?

There is then the miraculous antithesis between '**strings of steel**' and '**sinews of the newborn babe**'. Yet after all this torture, Claudius ends on an unconvincing half-line, monosyllabic, colloquial and simple:

> All may be well.

He doesn't believe it, and neither does the audience. But we have now been let into his innermost soul and seen his innermost fears. We will look at him as one of the damned for the rest of the play. And that is more disturbing than the sight of a plain villain. It would be too much to say that he has gained our sympathy; but we do now understand the hell that he cannot escape. We will now watch him dig deeper into it.

Since we have seen that Shakespeare's monosyllabic lines generally allow a straightforward and measured expression of emotion, we should note that there are no monosyllabic lines in this tortured speech until the very end. So far, we have seen Claudius in public or from Hamlet's or the Ghost's viewpoint. Suddenly in this scene, the play swings round and shows us the 'villain' from his own point of view. And this inevitably affects the audience's reaction to the next lines.

Hamlet Now might I do it pat, now he is praying.
And now I'll do't; and so he goes to heaven,
And so am I revenged. That would be scanned.
A villain kills my father, and for that
I, his sole son, do this same villain send
To heaven.

HAMLET, Royal Shakespeare Company 1965–6.
David Warner as Hamlet and Brewster Mason as Claudius.

At this point, Hamlet enters behind the King. We have already had some two hours of Hamlet procrastinating about the act of revenge. But now, he can actually do the deed, and the play reaches white heat. Hamlet's refusal here, when the killing could be so easy, is a deliberate shift on the part of the dramatist to move the audience's sympathy away from Hamlet. So here we see him prevaricating and excusing himself, but with very dubious logic.

Hamlet sees the King at prayer and says his first line to the audience. The alliteration of '**pat**' and '**praying**' gives absurd excitement to the line. It is too good to be true to discover Claudius like this. At the end of the first line Hamlet's hand goes to his sword and he says *as one line*

> **And now I'll do't; and so he goes to heaven,**

by which time the sword is drawn. 'Going to heaven' as said here is simply a circumlocution for death. And that is where Hamlet draws his sword. At the end of the action and at the end of the line, Hamlet pauses and realises what heaven actually means: redemption. There is no justification for the stage practice of breaking the line to draw the sword; it is written quite clearly so that after the line ends, with sword drawn, Hamlet reflects '**And so am I revenged**'. It is a thoughtful contemptuous line, leading to the second half of the caesura.

'**Scanned**' is a word that has often appeared in these notes. Here it simply means 'interpreted' or 'understood'. Hamlet is more concerned with what others might say – how they might interpret the killing of Claudius – than the primitive need for revenge itself. The paradox that Hamlet invents negates the ancient demand that blood must have blood. It seems a superficial reason for not killing Claudius at this moment, almost an evasion. It should be seen as such. He stands there, ready to strike – and then says that we must pause, with him, to think about this. It is a pathetic, almost comic moment.

There is a strong pattern of antitheses between '**villain**' and '**father**' and '**son**' and '**villain**'. The strong accent on the end of the line on '**that**' and the end of the line on '**send**' indicate a careful analysis that sets up the mocking reversal of '**to heaven**'. '**Heaven**' is here elided to one syllable, so that the whole line is only one iambic foot of contempt. There then follows a substantial pause while Hamlet considers his excuses and proceeds to more justifications.

O this is hire and salary, not revenge!
He took my father grossly, full of bread,
With all his crimes broad blown, as flush as May;
And how his audit stands, who knows save heaven?
But in our circumstance and course of thought
'Tis heavy with him. And am I then revenged
To take him in the purging of his soul,
When he is fit and seasoned for his passage?
No.
Up sword, and know thou a more horrid hint.
When he is drunk asleep, or in his rage,
Or in th'incestuous pleasure of his bed,
At gaming, swearing, or about some act
That has no relish of salvation in't,
Then trip him that his heels may kick at heaven,
And that his soul may be as damned and black
As hell whereto it goes. My mother stays,
This physic but prolongs thy sickly days.

Claudius My words fly up, my thoughts remain below.
Words without thoughts never to heaven go.

The next nine lines, up to the sheathing of the sword marked by the monosyllable 'No' occupying an entire line, are questions asked of the audience, which demand their approval. We may think that Hamlet definitely protests too much. There is something querulous and defensive about the verse. And we don't approve. Hamlet's father was killed full of sin because he had not confessed. He was not in a state of grace. By contrast, Claudius has been at prayer, has purged his soul and is therefore fit for heaven. None of this quite adds up. A murderer may pray, may indeed confess to his crime, but that will not stop him being judged in the next world. The audience are also aware of a further irony: Hamlet is refusing to kill Claudius because he has been at prayer. Yet the audience know that Claudius has been unable to pray. The irony is ridiculous. But then Hamlet's contortions of conscience are often meant to be ridiculous.

So, for reasons of chop-logic, Hamlet cannot bring himself to kill the King. He is prevaricating as usual. Claudius is ripe in sin, ready for damnation, and Hamlet considers this in nine lines of over-the-top rhetoric. If Claudius is killed replete with his sins – gaming, swearing, drunk or even in the pleasure of the bed – he will go to hell. The change of tempo on

As hell where to it goes

introduces the couplet. The rhyme not only gives Hamlet his exit; it stresses his last justification for his failure to do what he knows he should have done. It is this failure which prepares him; he then kills Polonius without a moment's hesitation. He needs to prove to himself that he is not the coward that he knows he is. Hamlet kills an unknown spy when he couldn't bring himself to kill a murderous king.

So Hamlet's rhyme threatens but prevaricates. Claudius' answering rhyme tell us that in his agony of guilt, he has still not been able to pray. The final irony is that if Hamlet had killed him, he would not have gone to heaven. He was not in a state of grace.

HAMLET

ACT 3 SCENE 4

Queen What shall I do?

Hamlet Not this by no means that I bid you do:
Let the bloat King tempt you again to bed,
Pinch wanton on your cheek, call you his mouse
And let him for a pair of reechy kisses,
Or paddling in your neck with his damned fingers
Make you to ravel all this matter out,
That I essentially am not in madness
But mad in craft. 'Twere good you let him know:
For who that's but a Queen, fair, sober, wise,
Would from a paddock, from a bat, a gib,
Such dear concernings hide? Who would do so?
No, in despite of sense and secrecy
Unpeg the basket on the house's top,
Let the birds fly, and like the famous ape,
To try conclusions, in the basket creep
And break your own neck down.

HAMLET
ACT 3 SCENE 4

This extract is towards the end of the confrontation between Hamlet and his mother and is the climax of the Closet Scene. The meeting has been long awaited. The son is at last able to accuse his mother and release his disgust (largely sexual) at her infidelity. This is mature Shakespeare, colloquial and stingingly dramatic. It is so outspoken, so abandoned that the sense of danger is frightening. This son will say anything to his mother.

What is more, Hamlet has killed Polonius by thrusting his sword through the arras when he hears the suspected spy. There was no prevarication then. Because of the rough treatment of the mother, the ghost of Hamlet's father has appeared and urged compassion. But Hamlet's convulsions of disgust erupt again. They seem to feed upon themselves.

Hamlet has just said goodnight to his mother and, seemingly worn out and repentant, has begun to leave the stage. Gertrude asks her desperate question, and there is a dangerous pause made by the missing half-line. Hamlet thinks. And then he succumbs to the temptation of arraigning his mother once more. He now speaks sixteen lines which define his feelings in the most graphic way. The verse elevates into dramatic poetry where the colloquial is cauterised by disgust.

The actor must first scan the lines, noting the irregularities. Again, any line that can be scanned with five beats, without the resulting inflection being false or artificial, needs to be so treated. Again, the degree of emotion (here, in my opinion, white hot) is a matter of the actor's choice. The disgust may indeed be expressed by these terrible words. But the disgust needs to be *contained inside* the actor all the same. Some lines scan well and easily; others awkwardly. The irregularities could suggest how difficult it is for Hamlet to keep control.

The first line is monosyllabic. It is watchful, careful, slow. The double negative gives a cutting edge:

Not this by no means that I bid you do.

The rhythm is regular but vicious, and the cross-rhythm on '**means**' (which is the unaccented word) gives a strange danger to the line.

The second line has an inversion, with a trochee on '**Let**'. The alliteration on '**bloat**', '**blunt**' and '**bed**' needs pointing. And there is a paradox to relish: this King is not called (as Kings usually are) good or kind or noble; he is '**bloat**'. A bloat King is almost

Queen What shall I do?

Hamlet Not this by no means that I bid you do:
    Let the bloat King tempt you again to bed,
    Pinch wanton on your cheek, call you his mouse
    And let him for a pair of reechy kisses,
    Or paddling in your neck with his damned fingers
    Make you to ravel all this matter out,
    That I essentially am not in madness
    But mad in craft. 'Twere good you let him know:
    For who that's but a Queen, fair, sober, wise,
    Would from a paddock, from a bat, a gib,
    Such dear concernings hide? Who would do so?

an oxymoron – a King without grace or temperance; a complete contradiction. Hamlet's hatred is intense. There is a hectic rhythm in the next line. The two verbs – '**pinch**' and '**call**' – both occur on the unaccented words, so making a cross-rhythm. Lust is near to madness.

But this line is followed by a perfectly regular blank verse line to re-state the rhythm. And it also delivers the profoundly unpoetic word '**reechy**'. This is a Shakespearean invention. The word literally means 'dirty' 'filthy' or 'squalid'. But here the assonance, or sound of it, extends the meaning. These kisses are sickening because they stink and taste of being sick. They slobber as they throw up. They induce nausea because they are about ungoverned appetite. The word is disgusting both in sound and in sense.

There follows an eleven-syllable line which the actor can only make scan smoothly by eliding 'with his' into one beat. If he does this he can emphasise and point the cross-rhythm with the word '**damned**' and the subsequent accent on '**fingers**'. Of course this man is damned: he is an adulterer and a regicide.

The rhythm of the next line inverts with the verb '**make**' so that the sense then falls on '**ravel**' and '**out**'. Both words need pointing by the actor: this is a horrible situation that needs defining. This is a perfectly regular line which prepares us for the change of pace on the subsequent caesura line. To preserve

But mad in craft. 'Twere good you let him know

as one line, and yet with a sensible break for the full stop, means that Hamlet must motivate this with cunning. He spreads the whole line, using its monosyllables. The monosyllables also enable Hamlet to take time over his great confession: he has been pretending madness.

A new tempo begins with the next line. The antithesis between a Queen and the creatures of witchcraft – the toad, the bat and the tomcat – is clear. All these animals are profoundly unclean. Hamlet's invective is as foul as he can make it.

On the following line there is another caesura break to allow two questions. Again it is a matter of the actor's choice; but in order to get the irony out of '**dear concernings**' where '**dear**' is both a term of endearment and a prohibitive cost, it is probable that the two questions should be run together.

No, in despite of sense and secrecy
Unpeg the basket on the house's top,
Let the birds fly, and like the famous ape,
To try conclusions, in the basket creep
And break your own neck down.

HAMLET, National Theatre 1975.
Albert Finney as Hamlet and Angela Lansbury as Gertrude.

There is more malice in the alliteration of '**sense**' and '**secrecy**'. And we then move on to the story of the famous ape. The modern actor, unlike his Elizabethan counterpart, will not know this reference because the story has not survived. There is a case to be made for cutting Shakespeare when his images or his topical allusions have become completely incomprehensible to a modern audience. But these passages are usually rarer than directors make out or actors can justify. The ape story is a case in point. This strange surrealistic image may be difficult to understand, but its implication remains clear. It also gives the play a moment of madness that is damaged by cutting it. Hamlet's arraignment of his mother then has no climax.

Apes are notorious imitators. This one steals a cage full of birds (his master's aviary) and hides it on top of the house. He then lets the birds out – perhaps imitating his master sending off his pigeons. Now the ape climbs into the cage and leaps out of it hoping that, like the birds, he will fly. He falls to his death instead. Hamlet is warning his mother not to open the cage of his secrets. When she jumps, she will not fly to freedom; she will break her neck.

To sum up the passage: it contains tough, muscular verse, not markedly end-stopped, but with a clear energy point at the end of each line which not only emphasises the sense but sounds manic. There is a little alliteration, a few antitheses, and two points where the tempo markedly changes around the needs of the caesura. Nonetheless, it is impossible for Gertrude to interrupt because the tempo is fast, fuelled by Hamlet's evident malice. His disgust empowers every image. The main task here for the actor is to keep the speed fast enough and yet remain coherent. The changes of tempo and the spreading of the monosyllabic lines will be a great help in achieving variety. They also give the actor opportunity to show how the words he is inventing bottle up and contain his malice. His emotions want to scream in disgust; but he contains them with a critical precision. Technically, it will be necessary to take constant breaths at the ends of the lines. Only then will the hectic changes of thought be possible to sustain.

MEASURE FOR MEASURE
ACT 2 SCENE 2

Angelo What's this? What's this? Is this her fault or mine?
The tempter or the tempted, who sins most, ha?
Not she; nor doth she tempt, but it is I
That lying by the violet in the sun,
Do as the carrion does, not as the flower,
Corrupt with virtuous season. Can it be
That modesty may more betray our sense
Than woman's lightness? Having waste ground enough
Shall we desire to raze the sanctuary,
And pitch our evils there? O fie fie fie!
What dost thou, or what art thou, Angelo?
Dost thou desire her foully for those things
That make her good? O let her brother live!
Thieves for their robbery have authority,
When judges steal themselves. What, do I love her,
That I desire to hear her speak again,
And feast upon her eyes? What is't I dream on?
O cunning enemy that to catch a saint,
With saints dost bait thy hook! Most dangerous
Is that temptation that doth goad us on
To sin in loving virtue. Never could the strumpet,
With all her double vigour, art and nature,
Once stir my temper; but this virtuous maid
Subdues me quite. Ever till now
When men were fond, I smiled and wondered how.

MEASURE FOR MEASURE
ACT 2 SCENE 2

This is a complex speech dramatically, but it is simple to analyse because it uses the same device over and over again: the caesura and the changes of pace (and thus of motive) that it demands.

Angelo is tempted by the attractiveness of Isabella to pervert justice. This tormented soliloquy reveals to the audience the turbulence of his moral questioning. It is expressed by an enormous number of caesura breaks where the mood and the pace keep changing on the first half of the caesura line. Then, after the playing of the break, the second half-line matches the first in speed and dynamic but not necessarily in motive. And once the caesura line is over, a new tempo is established with the next full line – a new beat. All these caesura changes are a perfect framework for a string of agonised questions that spring from a neurotic mind. Shakespeare has given the actor a complex series of changing rhythms and changing tempos to express the questions. The actor must find the feelings that are suggested by this tortured form.

Once again, the soliloquy is a direct discussion with the audience, made by direct contact with them. Angelo is telling the truth and hiding nothing. The rhetorical questions in the first line define, of course, his temptation. But they also challenge and involve the audience. In the second line, the key question is asked: whether it is Angelo who is tempted or Isabel who tempts? Who is the greater sinner? Then comes the admission that all the guilt is his. This honesty is expressed in weighty monosyllables.

The end-of-line accent on 'I' in this line defines the antithesis with 'she' earlier in the line. It also sets up, and gives the actor time to find and invent, the extraordinary metaphor expressed in the subsequent two lines: lust corrupts as it lies in the life-enhancing sun, like carrion flesh. Out of disgusting decay comes life.

The actor should note that having made this dangerous admission to the audience, Angelo's torment increases as he tries to justify himself. There are an amazing number of caesura changes of pace in subsequent lines. All these changes in pace are an eloquent demonstration of Angelo's extreme insecurity. The caesuras perfectly express a mind in torment. The contrasts are extreme: 'carrion' with 'flower' ; 'waste ground' with 'sanctuary'; 'foul' with 'good'; 'thieves' with 'judges'. And the greatest paradox of all comes at the end with Angelo's surprising confession: he tells us that though a whore has never been able to excite him, this virtuous maid, this near-saintly young girl has aroused him completely. For the actor to understand and endorse this complicated tumult of thoughts and feelings, it will be helpful first to learn the speech quite mechanically, marking and remembering the ends of the lines, and also marking and

MEASURE FOR MEASURE, Center Theatre Group at the Ahmanson Theatre, Los Angeles 1999.
Richard Thomas as Angelo and Anna Gunn as Isabella.

learning the changes of pace that are called for at the beginning of each caesura line. This is not always a slowing up; sometimes it is a quickening. It depends on the emotional needs of the two half-lines, how long the sense break at the caesura needs to be, and the necessity to make the two half-lines into one. The quickening cannot of course ever be done at the expense of chopping up the line. If the two halves are to be made whole, the second half may have to go quickly too – if it can. It will depend on the sense, and the agility of the actor emotionally.

Once this intricate shape is learned, it will be possible to find emotions which can induce and support it. The actor will find that the very complexity of the form he has been given will push him into a whole number of contradictory moods. If Shakespeare's notation is followed, the variety of tempo is assured and the warring attitudes within Angelo made evident. Shakespeare has taken care to keep the five beats of each line fairly regular; and the sense-break at the end of each line is precise and clear. This regularity offsets the constant pace changes of the caesura lines: the one supports the other. Technically, the speech is a masterpiece.

OTHELLO
ACT 5 SCENE 2

Othello It is the cause, it is the cause, my soul.
Let me not name it to you, you chaste stars.
It is the cause. Yet I'll not shed her blood,
Nor scar that whiter skin of hers than snow,
And smooth as monumental alabaster.
Yet she must die, else she'll betray more men.
Put out the light, and then put out the light.
If I quench thee, thou flaming minister,
I can again thy former light restore
Should I repent me; but once put out thy light,
Thou cunning'st pattern of excelling nature,
I know not where is that Promethean heat
That can thy light relume. When I have plucked thy rose
I cannot give it vital growth again.
It needs must wither. I'll smell thee on the tree.
(he kisses her)
O balmy breath, that dost almost persuade
Justice to break her sword! One more, one more.
Be thus when thou art dead, and I will kill thee
And love thee after. One more, and that's the last.
(he kisses her)
So sweet was ne'er so fatal. I must weep,
But they are cruel tears. This sorrow's heavenly,
It strikes where it doth love. She wakes…

OTHELLO
ACT 5 SCENE 2

Let us deal with a famous speech and see whether the clues for the actor provide any surprises. Othello enters the bedchamber carrying a light. Desdemona is asleep. His purpose, we know, is murder.

His utterance is public: he is aware of his audience. Like Hamlet, he wants to justify himself to them. He needs to kill, yet he cannot kill the thing he loves without explaining. He debates with the audience, using the figure of the sleeping Desdemona as the evidence of his jealousy and his sense of betrayal. His dilemma is tragic; and what he is about to do, horrific. He knows this.

He puns and quibbles on the word '**cause**'. Desdemona is the cause – the reason, the motive, the ground. She is the explanation, the occasion, the circumstance. She is also the business, the subject, possibly the court case, the legal process. Or her behaviour violates the code of honour: a duel is justified. Finally she is Othello's matter of concern, his apprehension, his justification; and the disease, the illness, the sickness. Shakespeare deliberately chose a very resonant word.

The first three lines are entirely monosyllabic – with the three reiterations of '**cause**' standing both as Othello's justification and as the opportunity he gives us to savour the contradictory meanings. The actor may indeed be able to use the monosyllables as a means of controlling the wild emotions inside him. The pace is deliberate, the control as hard as steel. The '**cause**' is of course primarily his justification for his actions. But it is also the disease, illness or sickness that Desdemona has exposed herself to by her assumed infidelity. It is secret and cannot be named to the chaste stars of heaven.

And on the caesura, with the last repeated '**cause**', the mood changes and his heart speaks. Still in monosyllables, he concludes that he cannot kill her. The whiteness and smoothness of her skin both prohibit the violence and provoke it. Her physical presence though brings him back to normality.

The significant transition comes at the end of the fifth line. Her beautiful sensuality must mean that she cannot be allowed to live; yet she must not be allowed to die because she cannot be brought back to life again. The agonising contradiction is shared with the audience while the sleeping body is shown to us. Desdemona is on the cusp of life and death.

The light in the room now illustrates the finality of life and death. If Othello quenches the light, he can relight it; but if he kills Desdemona, the action is an absolute: life will

It is the cause, it is the cause, my soul.
Let me not name it to you, you chaste stars.
It is the cause. Yet I'll not shed her blood,
Nor scar that whiter skin of hers than snow,
And smooth as monumental alabaster.
Yet she must die, else she'll betray more men.
Put out the light, and then put out the light.
If I quench thee, thou flaming minister,
I can again thy former light restore
Should I repent me; but once put out thy light,
Thou cunning'st pattern of excelling nature,
I know not where is that Promethean heat
That can thy light relume. When I have plucked thy rose
I cannot give it vital growth again.
It needs must wither. I'll smell thee on the tree.
(he kisses her)
O balmy breath, that dost almost persuade
Justice to break her sword! One more, one more.
Be thus when thou art dead, and I will kill thee
And love thee after. One more, and that's the last.
(he kisses her)
So sweet was ne'er so fatal. I must weep,
But they are cruel tears. This sorrow's heavenly,
It strikes where it doth love. She wakes…

not return. He apostrophises the light and he apostrophises Desdemona. One can be 'relumed'; the other cannot.

The first stage direction ('*he kisses her*') is in the Folio. The direction to repeat the kiss is a later editor's conjecture. Maybe Othello does kiss her again, or maybe he doesn't. It might indeed be more heartbreaking for him to find he is not capable of the second kiss. This – crucially – is a matter for the actor and the director. We must always remember that we are not dealing here with sentimentality but with tragic actions that are irreversible.

The later lines are all largely monosyllabic. The words control – or try to control – the emotion. The emotion is also highly sexual. Othello develops an extraordinary image: if Desdemona is capable of being in death as she is in life, he will kill her and then make love to her. The neurotic contradictions are horrifying. What is sweet is fatal; what is compassionate leads to cruelty. The speech winds to its end, knotted in paradox: this sorrow is found in heaven, but it is also a delight which is heavenly.

'Strikes' has many meanings. It is to affect, to thrust, to stab, to pierce; it is to steal, to rob, to touch; and most of all to have an evil influence on. An actor can get lost in all these contradictions, and the agony of them can only work if they are debated with the audience. Othello must know that everything he is saying is a paradox and that the pain of the contradictions cannot be resolved. This life is death, and this death is life. And on the brink of death, she wakes and lives. It is time to kill her.

By explaining himself to the audience and by searching out the cause in all its meaning, Othello makes the paradoxes active and more searching. The audience may still be bewildered rather than heartbroken by his credulity; but by sharing his soliloquy with them, he makes public the pain of his tragedy. The complexity of the form here clearly demonstrates the need for contradictory emotions. To some extent, the audience must share his anguish.

MACBETH

ACT 2 SCENE 1

Macbeth   Is this a dagger which I see before me,
The handle toward my hand? Come let me clutch thee.
I have thee not and yet I see thee still.
Art thou not, fatal vision, sensible
To feeling as to sight? Or art thou but
A dagger of the mind, a false creation
Proceeding from the heat-oppressèd brain?
I see thee yet in form as palpable
As this which now I draw.
Thou marshall'st me the way that I was going
And such an instrument I was to use.
Mine eyes are made the fools o' th' other senses
Or else worth all the rest. I see thee still,
And on thy blade and dudgeon gouts of blood
Which was not so before. There's no such thing.
It is the bloody business which informs
Thus to mine eyes. Now o'er the one half world
Nature seems dead, and wicked dreams abuse
The curtained sleep. Witchcraft celebrates
Pale Hecate's offerings, and withered murder,
Alarumed by his sentinel the wolf
Whose howl's his watch, thus with his stealthy pace
With Tarquin's ravishing strides towards his design
Moves like a ghost. Thou sure and firm-set earth,
Hear not my steps which way they walk, for fear
The very stones prate of my whereabout,
And take the present horror from the time,
Which now suits with it. Whiles I threat, he lives.
Words to the heat of deeds too cold breath gives.
(a bell rings)
I go and it is done. The bell invites me.
Hear it not, Duncan, for it is a knell
That summons thee to heaven or to hell. *(exit)*

MACBETH
ACT 2 SCENE 1

In the middle of the night of death when he is host to King Duncan, Macbeth awaits the bell which is the signal to do the murder. He imagines a dagger in front of his eyes which shows him both the means to kill and the way to the King. It is a sign that is literal and metaphorical. Like all Shakespeare's soliloquies, the nature of this dagger must be discussed directly with the audience. Hamlet debates in public his capacity for suicide. Macbeth asks the audience if they, like him, see the dagger.

This is mature Shakespeare, and his verse is now an instrument of infinite variety. He can move from the colloquial to the paradoxical and then on to the richly metaphorical with breathtaking ease. So the speech is by turns direct and plain, then convoluted and intricate. But Macbeth is always *telling* the audience – sharing his doubts, fears and imaginings. And the form of the writing tells the actor how the end result should sound.

At this point, Macbeth is a man in a fever, attempting to clutch a dagger which the audience can see is not there. Similarly, he is a murderer who may not be capable of committing murder. He is careful as he approaches the dagger – careful as he would be if he was trying to capture a frightened animal. It must not escape him, so he does not snatch at it. He has to make the reality of his imaginings and the reality of his silent castle into one action: murder.

First, the scansion. The first line could begin with a regular iambic accent on '**this**' or with a trochaic inversion on '**Is**'. It is the actor's choice; but I believe the haunted confirmation obtained by accenting '**this**' must give the vote to regularity. The line has an extra syllable – a tension point. The feminine ending insists that this is colloquial, not over-formalised speech. Yet the mood is slow, haunted. The dagger is not snatched, but slowly approached. Macbeth needs to stalk it.

Line 2 contains the caesura and so the first half of the line ('**the handle toward my hand**') will slow down even further to express its haunted assonance. '**Come**' and '**clutch**' provide the next careful actions, and they are expressed with hypnotic alliteration. The emphasis is obviously on the hard 'C's but even so the tone is subdued, trying to catch something that may escape. The faint rhyme between lines 1 and 2 ('**me**' and '**thee**') increases the eerie atmosphere. For Macbeth, the appearance of this dagger is a sign and a portent. It endorses what he wants to do, confirms that he should kill. So why can't he catch it?

Is this a dagger which I see before me,
The handle toward my hand? Come let me clutch thee.
I have thee not and yet I see thee still.
Art thou not, fatal vision, sensible
To feeling as to sight? Or art thou but
A dagger of the mind, a false creation
Proceeding from the heat-oppressèd brain?
I see thee yet in form as palpable
As this which now I draw.
Thou marshall'st me the way that I was going
And such an instrument I was to use.

MACBETH, National Theatre 1978.
Albert Finney as Macbeth.

There follows a monosyllabic line which is bewildered and fearful, slow and mystified. Macbeth has not been able to *touch* the dagger and yet he can still *see* the dagger. He can see it for us because of his tortured imagination. But we can still see that it is not there. The paradoxes proliferate.

The next line describes the vision as '**fatal**'; fatal to Duncan, even possibly fatal to Macbeth. Equivocation is always at the heart of this play. Nothing is what it seems: '**fair is foul and foul is fair**'. The opposite is also true.

The end of this line has the emphasis on the key word: '**sensible**'. A slight hesitation at the end of this line sets up the subsequent contradiction. This vision can been seen and yet not felt. Is it real or is it false? Is it a temptation which should be given in to, or a damnation which should be shunned? The emphasis on the end of the line prepares for all of this because 'sensible' means 'evident'; but it also means 'affecting the senses'.

There is a similar phrasing hesitation on the end of the next line with '**but**'. Macbeth is almost afraid to ask the question. What is it? He hesitates to say. And if the line is run on into the next, Macbeth cannot invent what he fears – the image of '**a dagger of the mind**'. Nor can he play the antithesis between that and '**the heat-oppressèd brain**'.

The '**dagger of the mind**' is a particularly rich metaphor. This dagger hurts the mind of him who bears it as much as it hurts the victim. Paradoxes continue. Is the dagger false? Of the mind or the imagination? Or is the dagger real? Whether it is true or false, is it a thing of damnation or an instrument of sacrifice? The paradoxes are resolved by a line which is made up of a half-line of three iambic feet only, all monosyllabic, all slow, all haunted. But we are now in reality, handling a dagger which is as real

As this which now I draw.

The action is suited to the word in the half-line pause, a pause which is specified by Shakespeare. In it, Macbeth draws his dagger. The instrument of death is now concrete. He will do the murder.

But the vision of the dagger is still there and it now moves in order to show him the way to the killing, like a deferential servant. And the following line affirms that the supernatural approves his action. Dagger is matched by dagger. The imagined becomes real.

Mine eyes are made the fools o' th' other senses
Or else worth all the rest. I see thee still,
And on thy blade and dudgeon gouts of blood
Which was not so before. There's no such thing.
It is the bloody business which informs
Thus to mine eyes. Now o'er the one half world
Nature seems dead, and wicked dreams abuse
The curtained sleep. Witchcraft celebrates
Pale Hecate's offerings, and withered murder,
Alarumed by his sentinel the wolf
Whose howl's his watch, thus with his stealthy pace
With Tarquin's ravishing strides towards his design
Moves like a ghost. Thou sure and firm-set earth,
Hear not my steps which way they walk, for fear
The very stones prate of my whereabout,
And take the present horror from the time,
Which now suits with it. Whiles I threat, he lives.
Words to the heat of deeds too cold breath gives.
(*a bell rings*)
I go and it is done. The bell invites me.
Hear it not, Duncan, for it is a knell
That summons thee to heaven or to hell. (*exit*)

The next line has an irregularity in it, which is a way of expressing the fear that now seizes Macbeth. It can be made dramatic by the elision of '**of**' and '**the**' into '**o' th' other senses**'. There is suppressed panic in the rhythm of the line. Throughout MACBETH, there is a conflict between the senses. What is may not be. What is seen may not be heard and what is touched may not be felt. The world is constantly dislocated.

Or else worth all the rest. I see thee still

This line is monosyllabic. There are two slow half-lines here, as Macbeth tries to pull himself together. But he is still hypnotised by the vision of the dagger. The blade now begins to run with blood and this both delights and appals him. To the audience, this is the moment when he is a lost soul. He now embraces evil as he begins an apostrophe to the powers of darkness. He becomes, in effect, one with the act of murder. By now he is certain of himself, calm and possessed with evil. The rhyme at the end of the speech affirms that his imagination is now silenced. He will do the deed. The doubts are silenced.

The antithesis between '**words**' and '**deeds**' needs noting and pointing. Macbeth is a man of action who at crucial moments is unable to suppress what his imaginings do to him. But once the bell rings, we are in the simple world of a man who kills. He prepares to leave the stage because the bell is not only the signal but the invitation – the reassurance to do the deed. Now there is no conflict, no more fear. Indeed, this man of action, having denied his imaginings, can even make black comedy out of Duncan's journey out of this life: he may land in heaven or in hell.

To Macbeth, at this moment, hell seems more appropriate.

ANTONY AND CLEOPATRA
ACT 5 SCENE 2

Cleopatra Sir, I will eat no meat. I'll not drink, sir.
If idle talk will once be necessary,
I'll not sleep neither. This mortal house I'll ruin,
Do Caesar what he can. Know, sir, that I
Will not wait pinioned at your master's court,
Nor once be chastised with the sober eye
Of dull Octavia. Shall they hoist me up
And show me to the shouting varletry
Of censuring Rome? Rather a ditch in Egypt
Be gentle grave unto me; rather on Nilus' mud
Lay me stark naked, and let the waterflies
Blow me into abhorring; rather make
My country's high pyramides my gibbet,
And hang me up in chains.

ANTONY AND CLEOPATRA
ACT 5 SCENE 2

Neither the eighteenth century nor even that most commonsensical of critics, Dr Samuel Johnson, could bear the freedom with which Shakespeare treated language. All words were his to call into use; indeed, he invented many hundreds of new ones. The French critics likewise could not bear Shakespeare's reluctance to accept a formalised poetic vocabulary which represented the taste of the educated minority. The reluctance to praise Shakespeare for his freedom with language lasted well into the nineteenth century. He was thought at the worst as vulgar and untutored; at the best, as a public writer who was obliged to pander to the tastes of the common people. It was not his taste, but theirs. From the Augustan age on, English critics established what words and what diction were suitable for poetry. And for the most part, Shakespeare was admired in spite of his diction, not because of it.

We are wiser now. Shakespeare uses bawdry, filth, colloquial slang, courtly delicacy, lawyers' language, seamen's language, the rough speech of soldiers and the chop-logic of politicians. He creates perfumed love lyrics, and then spins craggy and metaphysical metaphors. In his house of language there are no forbidden rooms. His characters have similarly eclectic attitudes. Often, in order to tell the audience their predicament, they use inappropriate language for their character – or what is at first hearing inappropriate. But it enables them to explain themselves, to tell who or what they are. Here Cleopatra can be shocking and deliberately vulgar, ornate and yet brazenly uncompromising. Anything goes because of the heat of her emotions; the fire tempers what she says. She is the great queen of Egypt and a fishwife as well. Cleopatra tells Proculeius (who has just captured her), that she is nonetheless invincible.

First, the scansion. The line structure is reasonably regular but there are four or five caesura changes of pace which show how provocative Cleopatra is being.

She taunts Proculeius and the changes of pace build to a climax where, as we shall see, there is a run-on to set up the crowning horror of the gibbet.

The first line is monosyllabic, measured. There is a deliberate challenge in the antitheses between '**eat**', '**drink**' and '**sleep**'. The mortal house of the human body can be destroyed by the self. Without food, drink or sleep the body can make itself die. Cleopatra will deny self-preservation. The great Queen will gossip away her life with idle talk and so avoid sleep. The change of tone and pace on '**I'll not sleep neither**' shows how serious she is, the mortal house is destroyed and leads on to another caesura change, and then another which invokes the '**dull Octavia**'. The competitive female is still alive in Cleopatra.

Sir, I will eat no meat. I'll not drink, sir.
If idle talk will once be necessary,
I'll not sleep neither. This mortal house I'll ruin,
Do Caesar what he can. Know, sir, that I
Will not wait pinioned at your master's court,
Nor once be chastised with the sober eye
Of dull Octavia. Shall they hoist me up
And show me to the shouting varletry
Of censuring Rome? Rather a ditch in Egypt
Be gentle grave unto me; rather on Nilus' mud
Lay me stark naked, and let the waterflies
Blow me into abhorring; rather make
My country's high pyramides my gibbet,
And hang me up in chains.

The necessary inversion of rhythm on '**chasTISED**' instead of the modern '**CHAStised**' makes the verb active and mocking. She now moves on to one of her perpetual preoccupations. From the moment that we meet them, Antony and Cleopatra see themselves as world figures displayed on a world stage. What they do, what they say, how they love, will be recorded and written about, argued over and relished for the rest of time. They see themselves as central figures on the stage of history.

So Cleopatra is haunted by the possibility of her humiliation in Rome. And here the contrast between '**censuring Rome**' and '**a ditch in Egypt**' says it all.

But antithetically, this ditch will be a gentle grave. Yet the image of being laid stark naked in the mud of the Nile until the flies destroy her corpse grows with clinical precision. She prefers to be a fly-blown corpse in Egypt than a figure strung up for the derision of Rome. The vocabulary is specific and it expresses a horror that she surveys unblinkingly. Further, there is a relish in the mud and the swarm of flies which is aimed at provoking the Roman. She seems to hope she can disgust him.

The inversion at '**lay me**' gives power to the shock of '**stark naked**'; and the half-dozen words that tell us that the water flies will eat her corpse as it lies in the mud are strengthened by the alliteration of '**Blow**' and '**aBhorring**'. There follows a strange and shocking transference of meaning. This last caesura runs on and executes one of Shakespeare's breathtaking changes of scale. We have been contemplating a fly-blown corpse, lying in the mud. Now we see another possibility; her corpse hung high on a pyramid, the chains dangling. We go from close-up to long-shot.

A small but important point can be raised here about choices in scansion. It's fairly clear that Shakespeare's scansion of the line was:

$$\text{My COUNtry's HIGH pyRAmiDES my GIBbet}$$

But we have never heard 'pyramids' pronounced in that fashion, nor would it sound anything less than affected to a modern audience. It is possible to scan the line:

$$\text{My COUNtry's HIGH PYraMIDES my GIBbet}$$

This gives five beats and an interesting cross-rhythm.

But who's to say what's right or wrong here? The actor and his director must choose. Lines must scan, but not at the cost of an affectation that will disturb the audience. And here the vision of the pyramid is something that cannot be missed by pedantry.

THE WINTER'S TALE

ACT 1 SCENE 2

Leontes   Gone already!
Inch-thick, knee-deep, o'er head and ears a forked one.
Go play, boy, play, thy mother plays, and I
Play too, but so disgraced a part whose issue
Will hiss me to my grave, contempt and clamour
Will be my knell. Go play, boy, play. There have been,
Or I am much deceived, cuckolds ere now,
And many a man there is, even at this present,
Now, while I speak this, holds his wife by th'arm,
That little thinks she has been sluiced in's absence,
And his pond fished by his next neighbour, by
Sir Smile, his neighbour; nay, there's comfort in't
Whiles other men have gates and those gates opened,
As mine, against their will. Should all despair
That have revolted wives, the tenth of mankind
Would hang themselves. Physic for't there's none.
It is a bawdy planet, that will strike
Where 'tis predominant, and 'tis powerful, think it:
From east, west, north, and south, be it concluded,
No barricado for a belly. Know't,
It will let in and out the enemy
With bag and baggage: many thousand on's
Have the disease and feel't not.

THE WINTER'S TALE
ACT 1 SCENE 2

Shakespeare's late verse can sometimes mislead the actor. He may get so tied up in its irregularities, its constant cross-rhythms and its tortured metaphysical language, that he gives up. He concludes that he may as well forget about the rules of verse and speak the speech for sense and meaning. But he is then liable to sound as if he is speaking mere prose; and then what he says will have none of the precise clarity of verse, nor the emotional pressure produced by the irregularities. Shakespeare could have written Leontes in prose if he had wanted to; but as he moves into his Late Plays, he becomes more and more fascinated by what extreme emotion can do to dislocate and deform regular verse. The dislocation is the result of *containing* the emotion rather than *expressing* it. Yet its jaggedness also paradoxically often expresses the emotion that is being controlled.

There is a further point. The speech may have wild irregularities, but unless the regular iambic beat is pulsing in the actor's mind and body, the shape of this late verse is easily lost. Shakespeare is writing complex rhythms which exist in counterpoint to the regular verse of his early years. Late Shakespearean verse takes enormous risks with the beat. His Late Plays were written to be spoken by a group of actors who had been living and working with Shakespeare's pentameters for twenty years. They must have been possessed by a rhythm that was an inescapable part of them. And this rhythm is always behind these late, almost dislocated speeches, making a strong counterpoint.

We are plunged at the beginning of THE WINTER'S TALE straight into the jealousy which is seething in Leontes' mind. His wife Hermione is, he is sure, betraying him with his closest and oldest friend, Polixenes.

His inner life is expressed directly to the audience and is in complete contrast to the courtliness of his public speech. He tells us candidly what is going on in him. By this extract, the jealousy is mounting. And there are three separate actions in the speech: Leontes watches the distant image of his wife apparently flirting with his friend. He also expresses his corrosive jealousy to the audience; and he succeeds, in some measure, in preserving normality in his speech to his young son.

The changes in this restless verse are constant. There are strange hesitations at the ends of many of the lines, and painful rhythms as extra syllables are crammed into his contorted speech. And all this is offset by bland attempts at normality.

Gone already!
Inch-thick, knee-deep, o'er head and ears a forked one.
Go play, boy, play, thy mother plays, and I
Play too, but so disgraced a part whose issue
Will hiss me to my grave, contempt and clamour
Will be my knell. **Go play, boy, play.** There have been,
Or I am much deceived, cuckolds ere now,
And many a man there is, even at this present,
Now, while I speak this, holds his wife by th'arm,
That little thinks she has been sluiced in's absence,
And his pond fished by his next neighbour, by
Sir Smile, his neighbour; nay, there's comfort in't
Whiles other men have gates and those gates opened,
As mine, against their will. Should all despair
That have revolted wives, the tenth of mankind
Would hang themselves. Physic for't there's none.
It is a bawdy planet, that will strike
Where 'tis predominant, and 'tis powerful, think it:
From east, west, north, and south, be it concluded,
No barricado for a belly. Know't,
It will let in and out the enemy
With bag and baggage: many thousand on's
Have the disease and feel't not.

'**Inch-thick**', in the second line, begins with two inversions; he is directly addressing the audience and showing the full scope of his jealousy. This second line is monosyllabic and it has an additional syllable. It scans:

INCH-thick, KNEE-deep, o'er HEAD and EARS a FORKED one.

He now masks his emotions to talk to the boy, with a reassuring instruction to do what all children should do – 'play'. But by the end of the line, the emotional pressure is too much. The emphatic '**I**' produces a slight break which delivers the irony of the difference between the boy's 'play' and Leontes' '**play**'. It also delivers Leontes to the audience. The subsequent '**Go play**' can be taken either back to the boy, or as an ironic comment, staying on the audience.

The obsessive repetitions of the word '**play**' – with its range of meanings from a child's amusement to a mother's dalliance beats in all these monosyllabic lines. The contempt and pain is in the alliteration – all the 'p's contrasting with the edginess of '**contempt and clamour**'.

The whole speech is informed with the colloquial ferocity of a man possessed. The monosyllables give it precision. The thoughts of sexual betrayal lead his racing mind into near-obscenity: '**sluiced**' (with the sibilance of the line expressing all the disgust), '**pond**', '**fished**'. The racing mind makes the phrases build so that the '**neighbour**' is first thought of as the fisherman and then named as '**Sir Smile**'. And the end of the line '**by**' sets up, with its slight hesitation, the invention of the name.

The caesura change of pace comes after '**gates opened**', and '**As mine, against their will**' is a phrase that surely slows up in its particularity to make a weighty line leading to the anguish of '**despair**'. The caesura break comes again on the change of pace: '**It is a bawdy planet**', and then on '**No barricado for a belly**'. The changes of pace show a man possessed, spinning out of control. The pace is hectic, but full of changes. The clauses follow breathlessly on each other and this long involved statement needs emotional punctuation. The rhythm is never completely broken, but it surges and pulses against the regular rhythm of the pentameter. The emphasis remains commonly at the end of the line and this makes the speech feel completely colloquial and spontaneous. Yet, the tumult of emotion enforces a change of subject time and again on the caesura, or on the dependent clauses. And the obsessive obscenities increase.

The actor's task is to unravel the form and define the shape of the phrasing and the changes of pace before any attempt is made to hot-up the emotions. The jagged nature

THE WINTER'S TALE, National Theatre 1988.
Eileen Atkins as Paulina and Tim Pigott-Smith as Leontes.

of the text produced by Leontes' constant attempts to control his jealousy when he needs so evidently to express it will be a great help in inducing the emotions as he begins to act them out.

All the hesitations and qualifications, represented by the line endings, the alliterative words, the caesura changes of pace and the inversions of rhythm have to be learned as a technical exercise, just as the text is learnt. This should happen before any acting is contemplated.

Finally, the mastery of this verse is that it is essentially dramatic. It ranges from the colloquial to the metaphorical, and yet allows a coarseness of expression which is at one with Leontes' coarseness of emotion. The speech ends with a climactic image of sexual horror. The belly admits no barricado but it does allow the entrance and exit of the male bag and baggage. This is a disease which leads to disease. There are no contradictions in this dramatist: he writes it as it is.

THE WINTER'S TALE
ACT 3 SCENE 2

Leontes …Thy brat hath been cast out, like to itself,
No father owning it – which is indeed
More criminal in thee than it – so thou
Shall feel our justice, in whose easiest passage
Look for no less than death.

Hermione   Sir spare your threats.
The bug which you would fright me with, I seek.
To me life can be no commodity.
The crown and comfort of my life, your favour,
I do give lost, for I do feel it gone
But know not how it went; my second joy
And first fruits of my body, from his presence
I am barred like one infectious; my third comfort
Starred most unluckily, is from my breast,
The innocent milk in it most innocent mouth
Haled out to murder; myself on every post
Proclaimed a strumpet; with immodest hatred
The child-bed privilege denied, which 'longs
To women of all fashion; lastly hurried
Here to this place i'th'open air before
I have got strength of limit. Now, my liege
Tell me what blessings I have here alive,
That I should fear to die. Therefore proceed.
But yet hear this – mistake me not – no life,
I prize it not a straw; but for mine honour
Which I would free: if I shall be condemned
Upon surmises, all proofs sleeping else
But what your jealousies awake, I tell you
'Tis rigour and not law. Your honours all,
I do refer me to the oracle. Apollo be my judge.

THE WINTER'S TALE
ACT 3 SCENE 2

Hermione has been falsely accused of adultery by her husband, Leontes. This speech is her defence at her trial. It has been a trial by threat and abuse, not by evidence. Leontes' syntax is tortured and irrational. Hermione, whose baby, fatherless, has been disowned and cast out, is promised death. A monosyllabic half-line continues with a matching monosyllabic half-line, as an awesome and heavy threat from Leontes is answered with Hermione's simple unaffected speech. Her sound is completely different from Leontes'.

The monosyllabic simplicity continues in the next line. The diminutive word '**bug**' illustrates Hermione's contempt. A '**bug**' is a bogey man, an imaginary object of terror in a children's game. The use of the word deliberately seeks to diminish this court and its hysterical King.

The ironies continue in the pun on '**commodity**'. The word means both a convenience and a situation that gives opportunity for profit.

Furthermore, the alliterative '**Can**', '**Commodity**', '**Crown**' and '**Comfort**' all need marking. '**Favour**' is the hyperbole at the end of the line, properly the thing she prized most in her life. It introduces a simple, monosyllabic line which goes through to the caesura break. There is a heartbreaking antithesis between '**gone**' and '**went**'.

The underlying emotion which Hermione is trying to control now increases. The clauses follow breathlessly on each other and the sentence has an enormous length as all her indignities pile one on the another. Yet this is a very controlled build and the actress must use the control in order to govern her emotions. If she indulges them, the text will become incomprehensible.

The strongly marked line-endings preserve the form in the mounting emotion. And the alliteration of '**Milk**', '**Most**', and '**Mouth**' leads on to '**Murder**' and '**Myself**'.

The temptation to run on at '**lastly hurried**' should be resisted. '**Hurried**' is deliberately at the end of the line and should be marked with a slight sense of hyperbole. Queens should not be hurried, they should be conducted. The word is picked out because it is an indignity. And the emphasis delivers '**Here to this place**'. Here again there is another cross-rhythm and an inversion of the regular iambic pulse.

                myself on every post
Proclaimed a strumpet; with immodest hatred
The child-bed privilege denied, which 'longs
To women of all fashion; lastly hurried
Here to this place i'th'open air before
I have got strength of limit. Now, my liege
Tell me what blessings I have here alive,
That I should fear to die. Therefore proceed.
But yet hear this – mistake me not – no life,
I prize it not a straw; but for mine honour
Which I would free: if I shall be condemned
Upon surmises, all proofs sleeping else
But what your jealousies awake, I tell you
'Tis rigour and not law. Your honours all,
I do refer me to the oracle. Apollo be my judge.

From this point, constant caesuras demonstrate that Hermione's pace becomes more changeable as her emotions become hotter and less controllable. She forces control on herself and is more deliberate in the simple monosyllables after the next caesura:

That I should fear to die.

There follows a piece of virtuoso writing. The rhythm is never completely broken, but it surges and pulses against the regular rhythm of the pentameter. The emphasis is commonly at the end of the line and this makes it feel completely colloquial and spontaneous. Yet the emotions enforce a change of tempo time and again on the caesura, or on the dependent clauses. There is a direct simplicity about this passage, a candid femininity which contrasts with the earlier emotional contortions of Leontes. By THE WINTER'S TALE, Shakespeare has achieved a mastery of dramatic verse which is unrivalled.

THE WINTER'S TALE
ACT 4 SCENE 1

Time I that please some, try all; both joy and terror
Of good and bad, that makes and unfolds error,
Now take upon me in the name of Time
To use my wings. Impute it not a crime
To me or my swift passage that I slide
O'er sixteen years and leave the growth untried
Of that wide gap, since it is in my power
To o'erthrow law, and in one self-born hour
To plant and o'erwhelm custom. Let me pass
The same I am, ere ancient'st order was
Or what is now received. I witness to
The times that brought them in; so shall I do
To th' freshest things now reigning, and make stale
The glistering of this present as my tale
Now seems to it. Your patience this allowing
I turn my glass, and give my scene such growing
As you had slept between.

THE WINTER'S TALE
ACT 4 SCENE 1

This extract is included to demonstrate that Shakespeare's use of verse remained varied and eclectic. To the end of his career, he used regular or irregular verse, rhymed couplets, four-beat lines, end-stopped lines, the lyrical or the metaphorical in order to give life to his plays. He used prose as well; but particularly in his verse Shakespeare remained experimental. He was constantly pushing at the barriers.

The Chorus of Time in THE WINTER'S TALE is in a sense a piece of impudent theatre. An actor comes on stage and tells us, the audience, that it is now sixteen years later. To help us accept this, he tells us that he is Time, and presumably he is dressed appropriately – with scythe, hourglass, and all the appurtenances of the Grim Reaper.

This short extract from Time's speech shows Shakespeare's mastery of verse. The Late Plays use verse in many forms. From the clotted painful searchings of Leontes to the youthful, lyrical effusions of Perdita, or the black magic incantations of Prospero, verse is now something that Shakespeare can bend in any direction.

So Time speaks in a strange, archaic verse, stubbornly and regularly iambic in its pulse, but with a constant counterpointing of the couplets, so that the sense units inevitably stop with the caesura rather than with the end of the line. It makes for a deliberate, chilling effect – like an unsymmetrical time signature in music – 5/4, for instance. The rhyme is inexorable like the ticking of a clock. And yet it is offset by the constant changes of pace demanded by the caesura lines.

Line 1 begins with an inversion, a trochee. The pronoun demands attention because this character must have an immediate command of his audience. There is an initial antithesis between '**please some**' and '**try all**'. But as the actor moves into line 2, the first couplet is completed by a record number of antitheses: '**please**' against '**try**'; '**joy**' against '**terror**'; '**good**' against '**bad**'. This character equivocates and relishes contradiction. It all needs pointing by the actor.

The third line is largely monosyllabic and gives importance to the name. This character is the personification of Time. '**Time**' is the emphatic word at the end of the line; and the line-break then allows a change of pace on '**To use my wings**'. It is a sinister moment: Time is inexorable and unstoppable.

I that please some, try all; both joy and terror
Of good and bad, that makes and unfolds error,
Now take upon me in the name of Time
To use my wings. Impute it not a crime
To me or my swift passage that I slide
O'er sixteen years and leave the growth untried
Of that wide gap, since it is in my power
To o'erthrow law, and in one self-born hour
To plant and o'erwhelm custom. Let me pass
The same I am, ere ancient'st order was
Or what is now received. I witness to
The times that brought them in; so shall I do
To th' freshest things now reigning, and make stale
The glistering of this present as my tale
Now seems to it. Your patience this allowing
I turn my glass, and give my scene such growing
As you had slept between.

The use of rhyme gives a deliberately hypnotic quality to the speech, but the rhyme does not force what is said into an end-stopped linear structure. The sense usually carries on to the caesura break. The actor will be tempted to run the lines on, but this will debilitate the rhyme and destroy something of the speech's deliberate oddness. Perhaps one or two run-ons can be earned if the sense permits it (and providing the audience is not given too much information to take in). But if this is the option that is taken, the stop on the middle of the line must be controlled. The primary use of the caesura is to dictate many changes of pace so that the mood is constantly changing. Allied to this strange form (which again is comparable to constant changes of tempo in music) there is a regularity of pulse in the actual lines. It takes a seasoned Shakespearean to speak this text and remain true to its ever-changing demands.

THE TEMPEST
ACT 5 SCENE 1

Prospero Ye elves of hills, brooks, standing lakes and groves,
And ye that on the sands with printless foot
Do chase the ebbing Neptune, and do fly him
When he comes back; you demi-puppets that
By moonshine do the green sour ringlets make
Whereof the ewe not bites; and you whose pastime
Is to make midnight mushrooms, that rejoice
To hear the solemn curfew; by whose aid,
Weak masters though ye be, I have bedimmed
The noontide sun, called forth the mutinous winds,
And 'twixt the green sea and the azured vault
Set roaring war; to the dread rattling thunder
Have I given fire, and rifted Jove's stout oak
With his own bolt; the strong-based promontory
Have I made shake, and by the spurs plucked up
The pine and cedar; graves at my command
Have waked their sleepers, oped, and let 'em forth
By my so potent art. But this rough magic
I here abjure; and when I have required
Some heavenly music – which even now I do –
To work mine end upon their senses that
This airy charm is for, I'll break my staff,
Bury it certain fathoms in the earth,
And deeper than did ever plummet sound
I'll drown my book.
(*solemn music. Here enters Ariel before; then Alonso,
with a frantic gesture, attended by Gonzalo; Sebastian
and Antonio, in like manner, attended by Adrian and
Francisco. They all enter the circle which Prospero has
made, and there stand, charmed; which Prospero,
observing, speaks*)
A solemn air and the best comforter
To an unsettled fancy, cure thy brains
Now useless, boiled within thy skull.

THE TEMPEST

ACT 5 SCENE 1

THE TEMPEST is a metaphysical play. In many respects, it is an inverted Faust-play. Prospero has made a pact with life which allows him to behave as God. It is true we only discover his god-like powers at the very moment he decides to abandon them. But who has damned him except himself? He lives a solitary life, locked in his own imaginings. They may be Art or Philosophy; Alchemy or Politics. But a sense of doom hangs over him and everything he touches. He has a daughter preserved from the corruptions of the world, a monument to innocence. Yet if she is to live and love, she must lose her innocence. His servant is the savage Caliban, a creature of primitive instinct and primitive power. Prospero represses rather than develops him. To allow him freedom would, to Prospero, risk chaos. Life is therefore held in an unnatural state of stasis. Without change there can be no life and Prospero remains consumed with the need for revenge. The wrongs that were done him by his fellow politicians obsess him continually.

Much like the confessional of Friar Laurence at the end of ROMEO AND JULIET, this speech is the confessional of Prospero. The regularity of the verse creates an atmosphere of invocation. Yet his plea is to release him from his sins. He confesses that which he wishes to give up. There remain many lines which nearly run on, then change tempo at the caesura and add up to an expression of Prospero's tension: he *needs* to be comprehensive, to tell it all. He must encompass the whole of nature, the whole of his living world. So there is a slow build over twenty lines to the first full caesura on

By my so potent art.

The second half of the line –

But this rough magic

– diminishes the potency of the art and admits its roughness, which means its incompleteness, its primitiveness. It is the opposite of that smoothness which Hamlet yearns for.

But Prospero is only a man, not a god. His list of what he has done amounts to an alarming series of boasts: Man is confessing that he can be god. And it is certainly a demonstration of the effort he has put into becoming one with Nature. He has had to make it obey his commands. But his potent art must be seen finally as blasphemy, particularly if he can, god-like, resurrect the dead, open their graves and allow the corpses to be reborn, as if it were the Day of Judgement. These lines must have been

**But this rough magic
I here abjure; and when I have required
Some heavenly music – which even now I do –**
To work mine end upon their senses that
This airy charm is for, I'll break my staff,
Bury it certain fathoms in the earth,
And deeper than did ever plummet sound
I'll drown my book.
(*solemn music. Here enters Ariel before; then Alonso,
with a frantic gesture, attended by Gonzalo; Sebastian
and Antonio, in like manner, attended by Adrian and
Francisco. They all enter the circle which Prospero has
made, and there stand, charmed; which Prospero,
observing, speaks*)
A solemn air and the best comforter
To an unsettled fancy, cure thy brains
Now useless, boiled within thy skull.

extraordinarily blasphemous in a fervently religious age. Those caught practising black magic were still liable to be burned.

Prospero's hubris brings on his punishment. He loses everything: his rough magic has to be abjured. After the sweep and energy of the great invocation, part filled with arrogance, part with anguished regret, the simplicity of his abjuring magic is the only way he can be shriven. The call for music is of course the crucial moment. For Shakespeare, music is the great healer:

> **The man that hath no music in himself**
> **Is fit for treasons, stratagems and spoils…**
> **Let no such man be trusted**
> (THE MERCHANT OF VENICE, Act 5 Scene 1)

It would seem that Prospero pauses and waits for the music to surround him. It arrives as requested. Prospero is demonstrating the supernatural powers he possesses at the precise moment that he gives them up. They heal him at the moment that he abdicates.

Mesmerised by the healing power of music, his enemies appear. Now it is their turn to be shriven. Their shrivings and their reconciliations with each other begin. The music rescues both Prospero's enemies and Prospero himself. With the half-line

> **I'll drown my book**

we are left with a pause. Solemn music heals the man who has committed the ultimate blasphemy. It also purges the politicians of their evil state-craft; Prospero shrives them as he shrives himself. He is now only a man again.

THE TEMPEST
EPILOGUE

Prospero   Now my charms are all o'erthrown,
           And what strength I have's mine own,
           Which is most faint. Now 'tis true
           I must be here confined by you
           Or sent to Naples. Let me not,
           Since I have my dukedom got,
           And pardoned the deceiver, dwell
           In this bare island by your spell;
           But release me from my bands
           With the help of your good hands…

SHAKESPEARE'S EPITAPH

Good friend for Jesus' sake forbear
To dig the dust enclosèd here:
Blest be the man that spares these stones,
And curst be he that moves my bones.

Holy Trinity Church, Stratford-upon-Avon

THE TEMPEST
EPILOGUE

THE TEMPEST mixes contorted late blank verse, comic prose for stand-up comedians, lyrics worthy of the early love comedies and colloquial intrigue fit for the politicians of the History Plays. It is a rich anthology of styles. There are also heightened ritualistic invocations which are sometimes majesterial, sometimes deliberately primitive. And to cap it all, the play ends with the direct naïvety of Prospero addressing the audience in primitive four-beat lines. Prospero and Shakespeare seem to be going back to a life uncomplicated by art or politics or love, and to be speaking directly like the Moralist in a medieval play. It is a deliberately spare and ironic moment, where the character becomes the actor and the naïve form supports him.

The simplicity of the four beats and the irony must remind us of a more absolute leave-taking: the four-beat rhymes on Shakespeare's tomb in Stratford-upon-Avon.

For centuries, people have objected to the literary worth of Shakespeare's farewell, but it is very akin to Prospero's, in metre and in attitude. There is a rich irony here surely. The voice of a man who could use words to create images to compare with the apocalyptic fervour of Michelangelo, the complexity of Rembrandt or the tumult of Beethoven seems now deliberately stilled. It is (like Prospero's last speech) the understated irony of the man who has done it all.

THE TEMPEST, National Theatre 1988.
Michael Bryant as Prospero.

ON A PERSONAL NOTE

When I took over the Stratford Shakespeare Festival in 1960 and began making the Royal Shakespeare Company, I received a letter which read:

> Dear Mr Hall,
> I am writing a book on the life and works of
> William Shakespeare, and would be grateful
> for any information you could send me.

I remembered that letter when I started to write this book. Why should I add to the mountain of books on Shakespeare? Well, I presume to think that I might be filling a gap. The techniques recorded here are historic and need to be passed on. So I hope this book will have a practical value.

Shakespeare has been a passion with me since boyhood. I need now to explain how this happened and why; and I need to thank the many theatre people who have encouraged me to pursue this passion. I have had the privilege of working with nearly all the great Shakespearean actors of the last fifty years. Their pictures are therefore in this book in productions that I have directed. What they taught me in the rehearsal room has been a constant inspiration.

School

In the Second World War, I went as a scholarship boy to an ancient grammar school – the Perse School – in Cambridge. At that time it was run on the all-male principle of the Victorian public school, with plenty of Latin and sport as the primary function of life. Yet there was one major originality: the teacher of English in the '20s and '30s had been someone called Caldwell Cook, now long dead. He had been a pioneer who was one of the first to recognise the potency of drama as a primary means of teaching. His theories were revolutionary and, in his day, somewhat suspect. The English, although they are very good at drama, always nurse a strong puritan suspicion of it. Historically, they have preferred to close theatres rather than open them. Even so, the pages of Caldwell Cook's book THE PLAY WAY still have life.

When I arrived at the school, small boys were still encouraged to learn about Shakespeare by acting him out in the Mummery, a damp cellar that smelled of leaking gas, and was situated under a Victorian part of the school. At one end there was a tiny stage. On it, we yelled MACBETH at each other, helmets engulfing our heads, cloaks over our purple and black blazers and wooden swords in our hands. Dressing up, telling

LOVE'S LABOUR'S LOST, Stratford-upon-Avon 1956.
Geraldine McEwan as the Princess of France.

the story and acting it out made it all come alive. To me the play was about black magic, blood, revenge, and – above all – sex. I was hooked. I was ten.

From then on, I force-fed myself on theatre – and whenever possible Shakespeare. I privately decided that theatre would be my career: that was where I was going to work. Turning out obsessive professionals can hardly have been Caldwell Cook's intention. But an ambition to work in the theatre is what the remains of his vision instilled in me.

I still think there is a lesson here: Shakespeare shouldn't be taught, he should be *played* – told as an exciting story. Studying him always risks ossifying him. Study is fine once the passion has been ignited. But that can only be induced by playing the play.

Cambridge during the War was a perpetual festival of the arts. Many productions toured there because they were evacuated from London. I saw HAMLET when I was a schoolboy. John Gielgud was the Prince and I stood at the back of the Arts Theatre for sixpence. I was there every Monday night. I also saw Donald Wolfit's whole repertory from Volpone to King Lear, taking in Touchstone and Shylock on the way. I saw the University's Marlowe Society perform TROILUS AND CRESSIDA. The text seemed almost incomprehensible, but somehow the author hadn't cared. It was my first lesson in the necessary arrogance of geniuses. We have to learn to dance to their tune.

By the time I was fourteen, I was journeying to London on cheap train tickets (my father was a railwayman), staying with an aunt in Lewisham and seeing Laurence Olivier as Richard III, Ralph Richardson as Peer Gynt, and Peggy Ashcroft as The Duchess of Malfi. Webster's ghoulish imagination was an early excitement; but Shakespeare was still what satisfied.

By the time I went to Stratford-upon-Avon in a school party, I was determined to be a director. Did I know what a director was? Hardly. But clearly somebody conjured up those stage images which haunted me for weeks. At Stratford, I saw the twenty-one-year-old Peter Brook's production of LOVE'S LABOUR'S LOST. It was magic – a gathering of young consumptive Watteau ladies and gentlemen in a drooping, dripping forest. How had he done it so young? I was very jealous.

I made my plan. I also (and the memory of this still embarrasses me) vowed to myself that one day I would run the Shakespeare Festival at Stratford-upon-Avon. I would try to get to Cambridge where I would read English and learn everything I could about Shakespeare. As a student, I would also try to direct plays. People did.

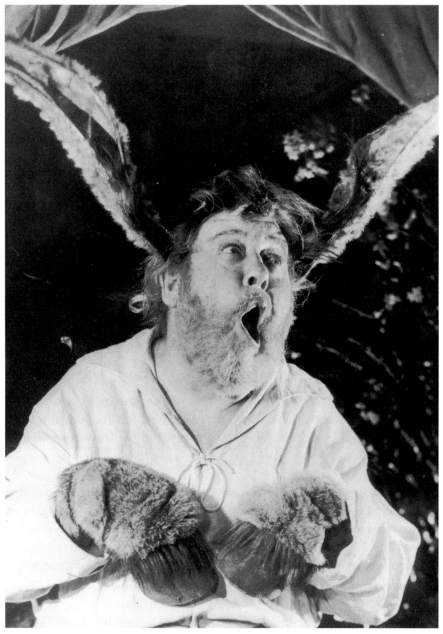

A MIDSUMMER NIGHT'S DREAM, Stratford-upon-Avon 1959.
Charles Laughton as Bottom.

To my amazement, and certainly to everybody else's, most of the plan worked. Two weeks after I left Cambridge, I was directing professionally. I have never been anything but a director. I must have been, I confess, a director before I knew *how* to be a director. If you are lucky, as I was, you learn by doing it. And I have never been out of work. This is not a boast but a mystery because in a desperately insecure profession I know I have been extraordinarily fortunate. I was certainly not born with a silver spoon in my mouth because we were poor. My spoon, if I'd had one, would have been wooden. But I had the support of two loving parents who believed in the supremacy of education as a means of getting on and getting out. Education was something that neither of them had had. If I was reading a comic, I was told to stop and help with the washing up. But if I was reading a 'proper' book, I was excused all household chores. I played the piano, read voraciously, and worked and worked to clear every examination hurdle, terrified that each one might be my last. The tension was sometimes almost unbearable. I am a child of the Richard Hoggart age – the product of scholarships and hard-won educational opportunity. And everything I learned took me further away from my parents. By the time I was sixteen we could hardly talk to each other.

It is certainly a blessing to have an obsession at an early age. But it is also very frightening and very lonely. The world may not let you do what you want to do. And you may not be capable of doing it. It is a terrifying time.

Cambridge

I was taught all the ins and outs of verse by George Rylands, the great Shakespearean of King's College. He was an amateur actor of note and an occasional professional director (he directed Gielgud's last Hamlet). He was also the senior mentor of the University's Marlowe Society – paradoxically the main presenter of Shakespeare.

My director of studies was the leading Yeats scholar of the day – Tom Henn of St Catharine's. He was also a prominent member, with Rylands, of the King's Group in the English faculty. They were romantic scholars of an almost vanished age; slightly precious poetasters all, and aristocrats of taste.

Their study of verse satisfied me but little else; and that was because the verse was a practical part of putting on plays with the Marlowe Society. The only lectures or seminars I went to were given by the abrasive iconoclast, F R Leavis. He was a radical and a leader of quite another group. His belief that a country's health can be judged by the health of its culture (and that complex art produces a complex society and vice versa) was as fervent as Matthew Arnold's. Art for him was well capable of replacing

A MIDSUMMER NIGHT'S DREAM, Stratford-upon-Avon 1959.
Puck (Ian Holm) and Oberon (Robert Hardy) observe the four young lovers (Edward de Souza,
Albert Finney, Vanessa Redgrave, Priscilla Morgan).

religion. Art was healthily ambiguous and undogmatic; and its integrity was worth any number of political movements. It asked questions and was wary of giving answers. But to my dismay, Leavis hated the theatre. He found it coarse and crowd-pleasing. In his eyes, it was a bit of a tart. I don't think he went to the theatre very much.

But he was a genius at analysing text, sub-text and basic intention. He could evaluate the integrity of an author by analysing the honesty of his style. Was he writing for effect? Or was he writing because he wished to indulge the reader's emotions? Leavis could tell you.

Subsequently, I found that playwrights often indulged themselves as the drama heated up – and that showed in the writing. When there was a clear opportunity to be restrained (and therefore often more powerful), playwrights needed to have it pointed out to them. It was and is a useful critical sense for a director to develop.

So I matured in the middle of two entirely opposing philosophies. Leavis led the Roundheads, and Rylands led the Cavaliers. Leavis taught me that theatre needed social commitment if it was to be at all necessary. It must always be careful not to become superficial in its quest for entertainment. Rylands taught me that theatre needed form if it was to be capable of speech. Strong emotion needed to be governed and shaped, not indulged. I went quietly from one faction to another; for the English faculty in those days was riven by a cold war between these two dons and their supporters. If my director of studies had known that I regularly attended Leavis, there would have been a very serious row. I was taught by polar opposites: I found it very stimulating.

Meanwhile, I was overwhelmed by England's new classical actor: Richard Burton. I saw him play Prince Hal at Stratford-upon-Avon. And in Paris, I saw Gerard Philippe, the new classical actor of France – in LE CID. Both performers had an economy of gesture and of speech allied to a wit which expressed a dry sense of the ridiculous. Together they seemed to herald a new age of precise, unelaborated speech. I thought that I was beginning to know what 'trippingly on the tongue' really meant. And these actors were teaching me. The older critics – as older critics always must – complained that these new actors were not poetic but merely prosaic. Their understatement was derided in both countries. But my generation – as the new generation always does – found them infinitely more 'real' and therefore poetic. To listen to either of them speak classic texts meant using your brain as well as your heart.

CORIOLANUS, Stratford-upon-Avon 1959.
Laurence Olivier as Coriolanus with Anthony Nicholls (Aufidius).

Burton's wry yet lyrical delivery led to Ian Holm, to Eric Porter, to Michael Gambon, to Michael Bryant, to Dorothy Tutin and to Judi Dench. Now there is a different generation – and there should be.

The revolution in acting style occurs every twenty years or so with predictable regularity. The defining actor of the previous generation has by now influenced all his peers so that his particularities have become clichés. They are used by everybody. It is time for the next defining actor to arrive.

Perhaps the biggest example of this change in fashion occurred in 1741 when the young untrained David Garrick took London by storm with his Richard III. The revolution is still amazing to read about. In my eyes, the Burton revolution was as profound because of his delicate treatment of the text. His Shakespeare was always linear but it was definitely 'smooth'. He spoke lines, not words. But there was nothing about him that was inflated or noisy. He was restrained, yet he was passionate. He was musical, yet never self-indulgent. His delivery was incisive and witty, it was (a key word for all us in the early years of the Royal Shakespeare Company) 'cool'. Burton's Prince Hal and his Henry V (a landmark to me but not to the majority of the critics) was part of Stratford's great series of Histories in 1951, conceived by the theatre's great director, Anthony Quayle. Audiences realised for the first time that Shakespeare had created a national epic which could make us understand the very strengths and weaknesses of our Britishness. These marvellous productions coincided with a boom in Shakespeare which was unprecedented. Stratford regularly played to full houses, as did the Old Vic. Shakespeare was suddenly big business and his energy fired the imagination of the country after the deprivations of the War.

The Professional Theatre

I left Cambridge reasonably equipped for my gamble and above all, thanks to George Rylands, the Marlowe Society, and F R Leavis, I left with an understanding of Shakespeare's verse and an ability to scrutinise it. It had been, all in all, an exciting three years. A group of us, led by the brilliant John Barton (who was responsible in my time for making Cambridge amateur theatre aspire to near-professional standards) had lived and dreamed Shakespeare. We had even learned to pronounce Elizabethan English – or what it was thought to be then. We staged a production of JULIUS CAESAR speaking it, and sounded like clones of Ian Paisley on a particularly cantankerous day. Northern Ireland was colonised at the time of Elizabeth and the Elizabethan vowels have stuck; so this was no surprise. Those vowels have indeed stayed with me and served to remind me when I read Shakespeare that his sound was rich and elaborate, with many

TROILUS AND CRESSIDA, Royal Shakespeare Company 1962.
Dorothy Tutin as Cressida and Ian Holm as Troilus.

diphthongs. It was not clipped and understated like modern English. The sound of Shakespeare's English is warm and resonant, paradoxical and witty; the sound of our modern speech is even and grey.

Years later, this conviction led me to direct a whole series of Shakespeare productions with American actors. This was not because I wanted to embrace the Method (a style of acting which was strictly non-verbal, invented for the most part by a group of great immigrant actors whose first language was not English and whose interest in theatre was emotional rather than verbal) but because I loved the rich sound of American speech. In its rhythm and resonance, American is much closer to Shakespeare than modern English. The American actor has a strong sense of pitch, of music and of pulse. He has a love of rhyme and of his native rich vowels. Consonants can bother him because precise speech is often confused with the affected speech of the aristocratic past. Being sloppy is therefore thought to be egalitarian and unpretentious. But without consonants Shakespeare loses his shape. Yet once the American actor is excited into a verbal commitment that is as strong as Frank Sinatra working the text of a popular song, then he can fulfil Shakespeare completely. The enemy is affecting an English accent which is thought classical, but which drowns somewhere in mid-Atlantic.

The Marlowe and William Poel

Judging Shakespeare by his sound is something I owe to the tutelage of George Rylands and – above all – the Marlowe Society.

The Marlowe Society was founded in 1907 in Cambridge and was inspired by the work of the great Shakespearean revolutionary director William Poel. In his day he was the scourge of Irving and hated his slow and sentimental speech and the elaborate and equally slow-changing scenery. In the eyes of Bernard Shaw, and of the founders of the Marlowe Society, Poel was the most Shakespearean director in the country.

Poel brought Shakespeare back to a bare stage where the audience's imagination was invited to produce images more vivid than the work of any scene painter. All they had to do was listen and imagine. The bare stage also allowed scene to follow scene rapidly and fluently, so that the articulation of Shakespeare's action – like a well-cut film, moving from scene to scene and making drama out of the contrasts – was again secure. Poel also revitalised the text. His mantra was constantly repeated as he endorsed Hamlet's requirement: the lines must be spoken 'trippingly on the tongue'. The quick and witty way was the correct way to speak verse. Irving and his colleagues

A MIDSUMMER NIGHT'S DREAM, Royal Shakespeare Company 1962.
Judi Dench as Titania.

had changed the fashion to suit the sentimentalities of the late nineteenth century. They had encouraged a taste for slow, sonorous speech. Perhaps, said Poel, this was the only speech possible for the new, cavernous gaslit theatres – those huge cathedrals of melodrama where the actor was hardly visible and barely audible unless he tore a passion to tatters. But this style was not for Shakespeare. I responded to all this – particularly the consideration of scale: Stratford-upon-Avon had a theatre that was clearly too big for its playwright. It was more like a cinema. Surely it was necessary to be able to whisper as well as to shout, if the full range of Shakespeare was to be appreciated?

Poel wanted acting spaces to be built on a human scale so that communication was always possible and ambiguity and contradiction always appreciated. His rapid, witty speaking technique had been learned, he said, from Macready's actors in the mid-nineteenth century. They had been taught by Kean's actors, who had been taught in their turn by Garrick's who had been taught by Betterton's. Then there had to be a stop because it is not possible to go further back. The traditions of Shakespeare's stage were destroyed by the Puritans when they closed the theatres in the Civil War. They stopped the greatest theatre culture since ancient Greece – arguably the greatest theatre culture ever. When the King returned at the Restoration and the theatres reopened, there was a fundamental change. Theatre had been a popular entertainment for all classes. It had been side by side with bear-baiting when it was at the Globe, and yet it was a place for the citizen's wife, or the elegant courtier. After the Restoration, it was for many centuries linked mainly to the plush world of the Court and the emergent middle classes. They wanted to be well-upholstered even in their places of entertainment.

When John Barton and I were at Cambridge, William Poel's ideas were still largely current and were shared with us enthusiastically by George Rylands. They had been the inspiration behind the founding of the Marlowe Society in 1907. Poel, Leavis and Rylands, although an unlikely trio, have in fact been the most significant if largely unrecognised influence on twentieth-century British theatre. A dozen or so directors, from Trevor Nunn and Richard Eyre to Nicholas Hytner and Sam Mendes, have been taught to analyse texts by using the techniques of Leavis. Poel's and Rylands' beliefs are also still current. Poel taught Harley Granville Barker. Barker was a great dramatist, a prodigious actor and the first director of international status that Britain produced. He is still the best commentator on Shakespeare's plays as plays; a keen sense of theatre is what characterises his eloquent PREFACES TO SHAKESPEARE. He played Richard II for Poel and Poel's staging techniques and particularly his verse speaking had a lasting effect on Barker. And thus on all of us.

top: THE WARS OF THE ROSES: RICHARD III, Royal Shakespeare Company 1963–4. Ian Holm as Richard III.
bottom left: THE WARS OF THE ROSES: HENRY VI, Royal Shakespeare Company 1963–4.
David Warner as Henry VI.
bottom right: MACBETH, Royal Shakespeare Company 1967. Paul Scofield as Macbeth.

Stratford-upon-Avon and The Royal Shakespeare Company

By the time I reached Stratford-upon-Avon in 1956 to direct my first professional Shakespeare play, I had a head full of theories and a heart full of hope. I knew, I thought, how Shakespeare's form could help the actor. And that he should work from form to feeling, and not from feeling to form. But I soon found that the imposition of form was distinctly unpopular among some of the younger actors. The Method was all the rage. Dicta which are pragmatic in the mouths of their inventors often become dogmas when applied by their disciples. So many thought that the personal qualities of the individual actor – his idiosyncrasies, even his madnesses – should be valued above the clear speaking of a text. 'Speaking' and 'projecting' (which is simply producing sufficient volume for the actor to be heard by the audience) were suspect. They were thought *unnatural*. So, I countered, was the act of standing on the stage. There is nothing real or true about learning somebody else's words and saying them from the stage dressed up as another *person*. Acting is not about being real, but about being credible. But a young actor can often become worried about outside disciplines that seem designed to make him conform – to make him appear like everybody else. This is particularly true if the disciplines are difficult to execute. He resists the challenge because he believes that his individuality is being constricted, if not denied. He also knows that individuality is his most precious commodity in our post-Stanislavsky, screen-dominated age.

So first of all, my Shakespearean aspirations fell on deaf ears. Formal disciplines are something that an opera singer, given the inescapable demands of the music, does not and cannot resent. It is actually impossible to sing Wagner or Mozart unless the breath is taken in the right place. Only after the breathing is learned can the performer say to himself: 'What kind of person am I? What am I feeling in this situation? What am I trying to express by singing?' The same need for mastery of form is required when an actor plays Shakespeare – or when he plays Beckett or Pinter for that matter. Any writer who communicates by creating a particular and personal form makes particular technical demands on the actor to express that form. It follows that an actor has to endorse and understand the form before he considers feeling it. To achieve this in my early years, I had to persuade rather than demand, cajole rather than insist.

Allied to this great desire for freedom, there were paradoxically a whole series of practices – formal demands – which were regarded as mandatory requirements for the professional production of Shakespeare. They were certainly not creative; most of them weren't even reasonable, but they were all followed slavishly.

THE TEMPEST, National Theatre 1974.
Jenny Agutter as Miranda and John Gielgud as Prospero.

First of all there had to be two intervals. It was believed that audiences would not last if an act of a play lasted more than forty minutes. Shakespeare of course wrote for no intervals and two breaks ruined his structures and increased the length of the evening to little purpose. It was also believed that Shakespeare must be cut. Audiences couldn't attend for long, and didn't understand unless simplification was the rule.

Stratford at that time still worked with a proscenium arch – a picture-frame. The only trouble with a picture-frame is that it demands a picture. Shakespeare's pictures are in his text. To put them on the stage as well is usually a distraction. And as pictures overstay their welcome, they have to be changed. Scene changes mean breaks in the continuity and music to cover the scene changes. So Shakespeare's rhythm of scene against scene was once again destroyed.

In rehearsal, improvisation was unheard of. So was any mention of verse: it was thought academic. There was a famous occasion some years later when the cast met for the first reading of a Shakespeare play on a Monday morning. When they returned after lunch, the director said that he thought that the experience had been so complex and yet so exciting, that they should read the play again. One of the leading actors was the great Shakespearean (and great individualist) Michael Bryant. Just as the reading was about to begin again, he interrupted. 'There is just one thing,' he said to the director. 'Are we doing the fucking verse or not?'

Usually we weren't…

At Stratford in 1956, there were basically three kinds of actor. There were a few old boys from the past who boomed and bellowed their sonorous generalities. You could hear what they said because they were proudly Irvingesque; but what they said had little meaning. They were extremely slow and devoid of wit. They did not speak trippingly.

Then there were the men of the '30s, bred on Maugham, Coward and Rattigan. They were smooth men certainly, smooth in dress and smooth in manner; but certainly not smooth in the sense that Hamlet wanted his speaking patterns. They threw their lines away with studied nonchalance and always wanted to appear 'real'. Their abiding fear was that they might look pompous. Emotional excess was curbed by the stiff upper lip and a studied geniality. Consequently they had a tendency to make all verse sound apologetic, like understated prose. This group was certainly shy of the classics and with good reason. The boomers and bellowers of the past genuinely affronted them.

CYMBELINE, Stratford-upon-Avon 1957.
Peggy Ashcroft as Imogen.

Then there were the young actors, Method-based and impossible to quantify. There were in this group as many accents, voices and rhythms as there were people. The new orthodoxy was that you must be yourself at all costs. And there was certainly little ability to speak Shakespeare. The discipline of verse was regarded as an unwarranted imposition; worse possibly than having to learn Standard English.

Contradictions at Stratford-upon-Avon

Yet other formal disciplines were accepted without question. Take 'blocking' – which is the imposition of the physical life of the play on the actor by the director. He gives the moves before the actor knows if he wants to move, or where to move, or when to move. 'Blocking' was, in those days, a measure of the professional virility of the director. The play was read on a Monday morning and then immediately put on its feet. The director gave out the moves he had worked out with the model of the set and his toy soldiers. And the actors carefully wrote the moves into their scripts. There was little discussion of motive or of meaning. By the Friday afternoon of the first week, if the director knew his job, and the actors got on with it, the whole play would be 'blocked'. The actors would then go off for the week-end to start learning their lines. It is much easier to learn lines if they are attached to a move, even if the move is an arbitrary one.

In 1957, I did my second production at Stratford – CYMBELINE. Imogen was played by Peggy Ashcroft and she was the first truly great actor that I directed. CYMBELINE was, happily, the beginning of a long professional relationship. We worked together some twenty-five times. CYMBELINE was also a road-to-Damascus experience for me – a lesson in how the formal solutions of theatre must transmute into the creative and pragmatic ones when necessary.

The last scene of CYMBELINE has thirty-seven recognitions – a father recognising his son, a husband recognising his wife. It is the great reconciliation scene of all drama; and if Shakespeare had wanted to have less recognitions, he could, by moving up one or two of the later ones, have reduced the whole thing to half a dozen. But he *wanted* to make it last as long as possible in order to show the slow and beautiful workings of destiny. The scene is ecstatic and surprising, disturbing and very moving. But it is an absolute pig to stage. All these fathers and sons and daughters are in the wrong place when they move from one discovery to another. So I had been very busy with my toy soldiers. On the Friday afternoon I was doing very well. The young director was dishing out move after move unchallenged. On one line I said: 'Dame Peggy, as you say this, could you move right across the stage?' 'Certainly' she said, writing the move in her script and suiting the action to the word.

THE WARS OF THE ROSES: HENRY VI and RICHARD III, Royal Shakespeare Company 1963–4.
Peggy Ashcroft as Queen Margaret in youth, middle age (with Donald Sinden as York) and old age.

I continued my blocking until the Dame's voice interrupted me. 'Pete, that is an awful move, I can't do it.' This remark induced pure terror in me. I knew that if she didn't do the move, the whole of my staging plan was in ruins. I could plead, beg, demand or order. But in my heart of hearts I knew she was right. There was a pause which seemed to go on for a very long time. Finally I said, 'Can we all sit down and discuss this situation because I don't believe in blocking and I don't believe this is the right way to work. We have been right through the play and you all have a framework; but it is my framework and not yours. More to the point it is not *ours* – which is what it should be if we were working properly and collaboratively. Can we go back to the beginning of the play and start again on Monday morning?'

It was agreed. And I have tried never to 'block' a play since. I always have a plan of moves worked out in case there is no creativity in the rehearsal room. But I always try not to use it. For the actor, it is the difference between dictation and discovery. Yet the form has to be respected even as it is challenged, endorsed even as it is denied. This is the paradox where true theatre is born. And I have Peggy Ashcroft to thank for helping me recognise it. Quite apart from this, it is undoubtedly true that without her support there would have been no Royal Shakespeare Company. She was the first person to join and where she led, others followed. She led the Company for the rest of her life.

I was offered the Directorship of the Stratford Festival in 1958, and my response was to suggest that I try to create the Royal Shakespeare Company. At 27 you have nothing to lose. Part of my belief was that only a coherent company could solve the problems of all the differing styles of speaking. Much has subsequently been written about the RSC's early aesthetic: how it was post-Brechtian, determinedly Left Wing, reducing Kings to ordinary men and making ordinary men into poets; how it was simple in its settings and often wilfully unemotional in its speech… Even if there is truth in some of these assessments, the main point is missed. It is true the Company generally shared a view of life and of the world. But the style of the young RSC was founded not on politics or design or anything aesthetic: it was the product of a group of actors all speaking the text in the same way and a group of directors who agreed that they all knew what to look for in the verse.

The young RSC had regular verse classes, led by John Barton and myself and some of the senior actors and directors. All rehearsals and all sessions were open to everybody, actors, directors, administrators, stage managers – and even office staff on a coffee break. This openness defined the Company, and was the most potent means of creating it; everyone knew what was going on. And the verse-speaking made the

top: OTHELLO, National Theatre 1980. Felicity Kendal as Desdemona and Paul Scofield as Othello.
bottom: ANTONY AND CLEOPATRA, National Theatre 1987.
Anthony Hopkins as Antony and Judi Dench as Cleopatra.

Company style. It quickly became famous for the clarity of its communication and the certainty of its speech. Plays became shorter because they were spoken more quickly. Audiences responded by understanding them better; and the theatre experience became keener and more lively. Many older critics, I suppose for reasons of fashion, were not receptive to our verse. So they were just as likely to condemn the RSC's new speaking as they were to praise it. But audiences found that they could understand the plays better, so they talked of the RSC's style and of its textual dexterity. Basically, it was a matter of generations: the old predictably found the new style unpoetic, the young found it rich and emotional. As I have said, such a reassessment is needed every twenty years or so. But the form itself does not change – only the way of expressing it.

After ten years at the RSC, I freelanced for a little and then spent fifteen years at the National Theatre, taking it into the new buildings on the South Bank. I, and others, did Shakespeare at the National. But in spite of some treasured experiences (particularly the ANTONY AND CLEOPATRA with Judi Dench and Anthony Hopkins) I always felt the want of a Company – a group of actors who shared an approach to the text and who were capable therefore of making all the disparate elements into a whole. There is no substitute for Company work. It is always the way forward in the theatre because it develops trust – actor for actor, and actor for audience. And above all it makes a shared technique possible. I am well aware, for instance, that the ANTONY AND CLEOPATRA was a delight because I had twelve weeks to rehearse – twelve whole weeks for us to find our way to a concept for this very difficult play. For concepts should not be present at the beginning of rehearsal. For a director to dictate a concept simply closes the minds of the entire cast. A concept of a production is achieved at the end when the group has done its work. That is why time is precious in the theatre. But with a Company, you can do in seven weeks what a disparate group will take twelve to find.

I have been lucky enough to work with nearly every major Shakespearean actor. I have learnt from them and I have had ample opportunity to test Poel's theories on several generations of actors. They persuaded Laurence Olivier to make more of the line structure; John Gielgud to agree wholeheartedly with fleetness; Peggy Ashcroft to delight in antitheses; and Ian Holm, David Warner and Judi Dench to relish wit in their own particular ways. When I mentioned Poel, Charles Laughton taught me the potency of alliteration. And I can still hear him creating the storm in LEAR in his study in Hollywood by pitching his voice at a level which a man would require if he sought to speak over a howling gale. I heard the wind in the silence of the room.

CORIOLANUS, National Theatre 1984.
Ian McKellen as Coriolanus and Wendy Morgan as Virgilia.

No great Shakespearean is without a voice, and I shall remember the passionate wood-wind timbre of Paul Scofield's voice to the end of my days. I shall also remember Ian McKellen's extraordinary physical presence: he seems incandescent on the stage. So actors have been my life and my help and my education.

And here is the end of my story, where uncannily it comes full circle. It is also where I rest my case. I have tried to define how Shakespeare's form can guide an actor. One of William Poel's most famous productions was TROILUS AND CRESSIDA. Cressida was played by a seventeen-year-old amateur actress that Poel took from a milliner's shop in Ebury Street. Her name was Edith Evans.

Edith Evans was one of the first great actresses that I directed. Evening after evening, I asked her to tell me the rules of Shakespeare's verse and prose that Poel had drummed into her. She said that I should think of them as 'Shakespeare's advice to the Players'. I understood what she meant because the demands she set out were clear and they were practical. And they were substantially the same as George Rylands had taught me at Cambridge. But then the Marlowe Society had been founded at the turn of the century on Poel's precepts by Justin Brooke – a distant cousin of Rupert Brooke, who was also a founder member.

Much of what Shakespeare asks of theatre people is common sense; and much, once the actor gets the rhythm of the verse pulsing in his head, comes instinctively. But it needs learning, and it needs passing on. The need to renew is also an absolute necessity of living theatre. Change is life. But you cannot escape Shakespeare's form, and you cannot alter the form. You can (and must) find new means of expressing the form. Too many modern productions mangle the text in an attempt to be spontaneous. The consequence is a lack of clarity and an audience that doesn't understand. Actors who are not supported by the form abuse not only their intelligence but their throats as well. They are prone to losing their voices. Acting Shakespeare is a physical, rhythmical and often musical discipline.

I'm often asked which I would rather see: a well-spoken production which observes the form but which is dead in that crucial area which always justifies theatre – spontaneity; or a creative production which is alive and which lets the text take care of itself.

It is an easy choice. I would of course always choose what is alive and creative. But the second choice is a contradiction. If the text is disregarded, the words become a secondary means of communication. The production can only then be creative if

ALL'S WELL THAT ENDS WELL, Royal Shakespeare Company 1992.
Richard Johnson as the King of France.

something else takes their place – such as music, mime or images. Certainly, such a production would not be Shakespeare, but only something based on Shakespeare. Shakespeare's beginning is the word; and his end is also the word. He tells you what he means, and therefore what he means you to feel. And – if you are an actor – he tells you how to *shape* the words.

Some years ago, the National Theatre Studio did a series of Workshops at the Edinburgh Festival. I was told of a conversation between a young man and his girlfriend who were signing up for a number of sessions. As they finished, the girl suddenly said: 'O look, Peter Hall's doing a Workshop session on Shakespeare's verse. I want to go to that'. Her partner looked at her in amazement. 'You don't want to go to that,' he said. 'He is an iambic fundamentalist.' I remain very flattered.

HAMLET, Peter Hall Company at the Gielgud Theatre 1994.
Stephen Dillane as Hamlet.

LIST OF ILLUSTRATIONS

ALSO BY PETER HALL
published by Oberon Books

Exposed by the Mask
Form and Language in Drama

In these four lectures Peter Hall reveals a lifetime's discoveries about classical theatre, Shakespeare, opera and modern drama. The central argument is that form and structured language paradoxically give freedom to power of thought and feeling, much as the masks of early Greek drama enabled actors to express extreme emotion. The mask may take many forms – the precise language of Beckett and Pinter, the classical form of Mozart's operas, or Shakespeare's verse.

ISBN 1 84002 182 9
paperback £7.99

The Autobiography of Peter Hall
Making an Exhibition of Myself

The story of a railway worker's son who became one of the most powerful, outspoken and charismatic figures in European theatre.

'It becomes a classic story…of an outsider who, through talent, energy and doggedness, fights his way to the inside…an unusually honest book'
Michael Billington

ISBN 1 84002 115 2
paperback £12.99

Peter Hall's Diaries
The Story of a Dramatic Battle

The diaries cover the period from 1972 to 1980, during which Peter Hall oversaw the historic move of the National Theatre from the Old Vic to the South Bank. He vividly recounts eight years of intense creativity, through all the triumphs and frustrations of 'a kind of war I had to win'. He reveals uniquely what it is like to be head of a great artistic enterprise struggling to establish itself under intense public scrutiny.

ISBN 1 84002 102 0
paperback £15.99

www.oberonbooks.com